Praise for *Give Me a Word*

"Christine Valters Paintner's warm-hearted, beautiful *Give Me a Word* welcomes us into wise, gentle activities for embracing radical simplicity in our day-to-day lives, in community with others. Reading it feels like a desert amma or abba turned up where you live, rapped on your door, handed you a papyrus scroll, and said: 'Heard you've been asking for a map to my cave. Visit anytime for a word.' Highly recommend it to anyone wanting to live in and from the calm and compassionate intersection of time and eternity!"

—**Carmen Acevedo Butcher**, PhD, poet and award-winning translator of *The Cloud of Unknowing*, *Practice of the Presence* by Brother Lawrence, and works by Hildegard of Bingen

"I love this book! In *Give Me a Word*, Christine Valters Paintner takes the reader on a thirty-day pilgrimage to search for, acquire, and carry a word for a year. Based on an ancient practice of asking for and receiving a guiding word, this beautifully written spiritual classic overflows with transformative and heart-centered meditations, spiritual practices, and reflections from people who journeyed through this divine adventure.

An excellent book for spiritual groups of all kinds. *Give Me a Word* is a gift to the entire spiritual community."

—**Lerita Coleman Brown**, PhD, spiritual companion, speaker, and author of *What Makes You Come Alive: A Spiritual Walk with Howard Thurman*

"*Give Me a Word* is a seedbed of insight, wisdom, practices, and lived experience. This inviting text leads the reader to gently dwell in silence, receive the implanted word and savor the embodied life that desert wisdom offers. Be prepared for creative and surprising possibilities! While good company for the solitary reader, it is also a lovely guide for group formation. Highly recommended."

—**Mary C. Earle**, author of *The Desert Mothers: Spiritual Practices from the Women of the Wilderness*

"In *Give Me a Word,* Paintner not only guides the reader to the point of choosing their own word of life but also invites them into dancing with that word throughout the year. With ancient practices and creative counsel, this book is a constant balm for every ache, joy, and longing along the way."

—**Cassidy Hall**, author of *Queering Contemplation*, cohost of the *Encountering Silence* podcast, and creator of the *Contemplating Now* and *Queering Contemplation* podcasts

"Christine Valters Paintner has done us all a huge service by assembling the best of the best of life-giving spiritual practices that serve to nourish our heart's deep hunger for wisdom. *Give Me a Word* is a vast treasure trove of both ancient and contemporary spiritual resources that are simultaneously insightful, creative, and, above all, highly practical! Partaking in and of them can only prove to be a rich endeavor of the soul."

—**Wil Hernandez**, PhD, Obl. OSB, executive director of CenterQuest; author of *Accidental Monk: A Chronicle of Struggle, Faith, and Surrender* and a trilogy of books on Henri Nouwen

"In my studies with Christine Valters Paintner, I've learned a great deal about the one-word practice, and I use her valuable insights in engaging with the practice both at the turn of a new year and at various junctures throughout. I am delighted that these teachings are now available in book form with *Give Me a Word*. Christine possesses a unique gift for bringing ancient, Christian contemplative wisdom into the present for those of us navigating the realities of modern life. I highly recommend *Give Me a Word* and will be regularly recommending it to my students and those I serve."

—**Dr. Jamie Marich**, author of *You Lied to Me About God: A Memoir* and *Dissociation Made Simple*, and founder of The Institute for Creative Mindfulness

"Every chapter in Christine Valters Paintner's *Give Me a Word*, and her guided meditations included throughout the book, are grace-filled invitations that not only remind us, but even *equip* us, to bring our awareness from our mind to our heart, and to live from 'this place of receptivity and intuition.' See if, like me, your day-to-day perspective is changed in delightful and important ways, enabling you to be more aware, more oriented toward an expanded sense of *noticing*—noticing the Divine in your everyday life, the seasons and thresholds of your life, and the shimmering presence of Love everywhere. I will always hold *Give Me a Word* close to my heart in gratitude for its soul-filling wisdom and practical instruction on how to wake up to the Mystery within and all around us, beckoning us to live the life we are meant to live. You will not want to miss reading this treasure of a book!"

—**Caroline Oakes**, author of *Practice the Pause: Jesus' Contemplative Practice, New Brain Science, and What It Means to Be Fully Human*

"Christine Valters Paintner's *Give Me a Word* is another of her many books offering rich spiritual guidance. It is based on the wisdom of the early fathers and mothers of the desert who often heard from those who sought them out, 'Give me a word'—a word to reflect upon, perhaps for a day, possibly a lifetime. Paintner invites her readers to consider, in their quiet or still moments, sacred texts, dreams, nature, the body, soul friends, ancestors. She offers, not esoteric, but very practical advice that encourages and may lead to unexpected awakenings, epiphanies, transformations. I cannot recommend this book highly enough to anyone who is searching for a new direction in their life or a deepening of the life they are already leading."

—**Ed Sellner**, professor emeritus of theology and spirituality, St. Catherine University, St. Paul, Minnesota, and author of numerous books including *Celtic Saints and Their Animal Friends: A Spiritual Kinship*

"*Give Me a Word* is the best book on *lectio divina* I've encountered. Christine Valters Paintner's process is unique and creative. She takes her readers on a pilgrimage over thirty days with a received word, delineating creative ways to savor and deepen and experience that year's received word. I love her progression. She ends each 'day' with examples shared by past participants. I highly recommend this!"

—**Laura Swan**, OSB, author of *The Forgotten Desert Mothers: Sayings, Lives, and Stories of Early Christian Women*

"This book helped me feel the difference between the din and the hum of the world. With its help, I'm learning to quiet the one and embrace the other."

—**Jon M. Sweeney**, author of *The Complete Francis of Assisi* and *Sit in the Sun*

"Christine Valters Paintner's *Give Me a Word* is a creative, heart-centered invitation to listen to and live your life differently. As in the case of the *ammas* and *abbas* of the fourth and fifth century, we are being asked to find a 'word' to guide us toward greater inner freedom going forth. This process is dramatic because it will require us to surface the words (discouragement, loneliness, misunderstanding, fear, loss, rejection, anger, regret, confusion, or boredom) that may be limiting us now without our even being aware of it. Also, in searching in a deeper way for an enriching word by viewing the messages that others, nature, reading, sacred scripture, and our own intuition may be offering us, we will realize that it is a dynamic, never-ending process. The wisdom that arises from combining humility with knowledge can never be possessed but must be received again and again as we cross different psychological and spiritual thresholds. Fortunately, finding a word and letting its power deepen until it needs to be transformed into another one now has a simple, beautiful, wise, and instructive guide: Christine Valters Paintner's *Give Me a Word.* Reading it was like being on a week's retreat on discovering new inner peace, greater personal joy, and a way to let compassion be a circle of grace for us and those who need a healthier sense of our presence in their lives."

—**Robert J. Wicks,** author of *The Simple Care of a Hopeful Heart: Mentoring Yourself in Difficult Times*, professor emeritus, Loyola University Maryland

Give Me a Word

CHRISTINE VALTERS PAINTNER

Give Me a Word

The Promise of an Ancient Practice to Guide Your Year

Broadleaf Books
Minneapolis

GIVE ME A WORD
The Promise of an Ancient Practice to Guide Your Year

31 30 29 28 27 26 25 1 2 3 4 5 6 7 8 9

Library of Congress Cataloging-in-Publication Data

Names: Paintner, Christine Valters, author.
Title: Give me a word : the promise of an ancient practice to guide your year / Christine Valters Paintner.
Description: Minneapolis : Broadleaf Books, [2025] | Includes bibliographical references.
Identifiers: LCCN 2024052149 | ISBN 9798889831266 (hardback) | ISBN 9798889831273 (ebook)
Subjects: LCSH: Spiritual direction—Christianity. | Christian life—Meditations.
Classification: LCC BV5053 .P35 2025 | DDC 248/.4—dc23/eng/20250109
LC record available at https://lccn.loc.gov/2024052149

Cover design by Studio Gearbox

Print ISBN: 979-8-8898-3126-6
eBook ISBN: 979-8-8898-3127-3

Printed in China

For all the ancient and contemporary wild-hearted ammas and abbas who let the desert work its power and who listen for the sacred word of Mystery to emerge from within

Contents

Part Two: Receiving the Word

Part Three: Carry the Word with You

Introduction

Every year before Christmas since 2008, I have posted an invitation on our Abbey of the Arts website, inviting people to listen for a word to guide them in the year ahead. I share a few simple practices for listening and then ask them to share their word with the community. This has become a popular offering each year, something people look forward to, and hundreds of people participate.

The practices are not about resolutions or goal-setting; they are not about achieving more in the new year or accomplishing tasks or checking things off a list. They are about listening for what is calling to you in a particular season of life. They ask us to trust a greater wisdom at work in the world than our own egos.

The word might be a single word or a phrase, or it might even be an image. This practice has been growing in popularity in recent years but is often divorced from its ancient roots. It originates from the wisdom of the desert fathers and mothers, those elders who, in the second and third centuries, went to the deserts of Egypt, Syria, and Palestine to cultivate a life of radical simplicity and ongoing devotion to the presence of the divine in their lives.

A key phrase often repeated in the sayings of the desert mothers and fathers is "give me a word." When a novice approaches one of the *ammas* or *abbas* and says, "Give me a word," "he or she is not asking for either a command or a solution, but for a communication that can be received as a stimulus to grow into fuller life. It is never a theoretical matter, and the elders are scathing about those who want simply something to discuss." Here is one story from the desert father Hierax: "A brother questioned Abba Hierax saying, 'Give me a word. How can I be saved?' The old man said to him, 'Sit in your cell, and if you are hungry, eat, if you are thirsty, drink; only do not speak evil of anyone, and you will be saved.'"

We find this phrase repeated throughout the stories of the desert elders. This tradition of asking for a word was a way of seeking something on which to ponder for many days, weeks, months, sometimes a whole lifetime. A "word" was often a short phrase to nourish and challenge the receiver. A word was meant to be wrestled with and slowly grown into: "A monk once came to Basil of Caesarea and said, 'Speak a word, Father'; and Basil replied, 'Thou shalt love the Lord thy God with all thy heart,' and the monk went away at once. Twenty years later, he came back and said, 'Father, I have struggled to keep your word; now speak another word to me'; and he said, 'Thou shalt love thy neighbor as thyself'; and the monk returned in obedience to his cell to keep that also." This story demonstrates how a word could be worked on for years at a time. The word being sought was not a theological explanation or counseling. It was part of a relationship that had developed with the assumption that this word, when received by the disciple, would be life-giving. It was meant for this person in this moment and season of their lives.

As you begin this journey of listening for your word, release your thinking mind and enter into a space of receiving. Ask the wise presences in your life for your own life-giving word. You will be invited to listen in the stillness to sacred texts, to your life, to dreams, to nature, to your body, to soul friends, to the ancestors. The word might come from reading a poem or story. It might come in a time of stillness, or it might arrive as wise words offered from an unexpected source, a dream symbol, a line from a conversation, or an image you stumble across that seizes your imagination.

I often ask for a word as I take my daily walks. I listen for what the trees and pigeons might have to offer me. When we receive a word, often it is confirmed through synchronicities that continue to appear to us or a sense of felt rightness.

I sometimes describe this process of listening as looking for what shimmers. *Shimmering* is a way to describe when something in the world is calling to you, beckoning you, sometimes even urging you to pay closer attention. Sometimes what shimmers is challenging, but we know that wrestling with it will yield something bigger in our lives. Sometimes what shimmers invokes wonder and awe. We notice a felt response in our bodies and spirits that asks us to attune more deeply to what is being revealed.

The purpose of the word is to simply hold it in your heart, turning it over and over, pondering but not analyzing. Give it space within you to speak. Once a word does arrive, we don't force it into a meaning for us. We let it unfold slowly.

This book is an invitation to a set of practices that will help you cultivate this receptive stance so you can receive a word. This is the focus of part one. Once the word arrives, in part two, I offer you some ways to help confirm the word and further break open its meaning through creative explorations. Finally, in part three, I invite you to make some commitments for the season ahead rooted in your word.

I recommend choosing a day to begin and then reading and practicing one day at a time for thirty days. If you are engaging this process as a New Year's ritual, you might begin at the start of Advent or December, but it can be done any other time of year as well, whenever you feel yourself entering a new season of life and could use some direction and guidance. The word can be an anchor or like a talisman or compass.

Remember that this is a slow process of unfolding and receiving, not something to rush through and grasp for. We are attuning ourselves to a different way of being in the world. I recommend, after each day's practice, to allow some time for reflective writing where you write any images or feelings that came to you. This works best as a time of freewriting without editing. You are not writing to create a product but for the process of discovery that happens when we set our internal editor aside and listen to what has been stirring in our hearts.

If, after the first ten days, a word has not yet arrived, consider staying with those first few practices and repeating them as needed. There is no rush to arrive.

In the pages that follow, I will also share some of the words that have nourished me over the years and how I have let them shape me, along with some inspiration members of the Abbey of the Arts community have offered over the years.

Some of the words our community members have received through this process include the following:

space	release
richness	presence
goodness	listen
connection (with self and others)	awakening
	balance
awareness	wisdom
woven	healing
luminous	incarnation
silence	embodiment
mercy	depth
embrace	receive
amazement	playfulness
well-being	reveal
grounded	gather
pray	and many more!

Here are a few reflections on the words that chose some of our participants:

> Being really true to self, authentic comes to mind—staying strong and determined with deep truth in everything I do. (Barry Carter Gibby)

My word for the year is *leichtigkeit* (facility, ease). Related to favor and grace. But there is also some connection to the spiritual gift for the Enneagram One, which Richard Rohr calls *heitere Gelassenheit* in the German translation (serenity in the original). So I'm looking forward to a year of facility, favor, and serenity. (Jutta Blühberger)

My word for 2024 is "Allow the Light." Allow the light to shine for me, through me, from me. Allow the light of others to reach me. Allow me to feel the light of source. And more! (Debra Olson-Tolar)

Moonlight—embrace the shimmering, soft streams. Honor the moonbeam that is an older, wiser me. (Ellis Sanford)

Playfulness—to counter all that perceived need to take the path with God as a serious endeavour alone. (Gia Daprano)

Threshold is my word for 2024. For me it will be a year of a significant move, leaving a home of 30 years and into a new one in a contemplative community near a Benedictine monastery. Hence a physical threshold but also an emotional and spiritual threshold, all of which will be challenging. (Barbara Neilon)

I hope these begin to stir your imagination about the possibilities awaiting you.

Prelude

Savor

In 2012, the word that claimed me for the year was *savor.* I had been reading *In the Company of Rilke* by Stephanie Dowrick. The German poet Rilke has been a teacher of mine for many years, but that previous year, his wisdom became even more necessary for my life. Each morning as a part of my daily prayer and journaling time, I read a poem of his in German and did my best to translate with my rusty language skills. Then I read the translation offered to see which nuances I might have missed.

Then I let a kind of *lectio divina* practice unfold in my prayer, where I listen for a word or phrase that shimmers and then sit with what it has to reveal to me. Sometimes the meaning emerges quickly in the silence; often, it ripens over many days. As I read in Dowrick's book, she was exploring how a central motivation of Rilke's poetry is to ponder what it means to live this human life we are given, to discover the inner nature of one's particular experience. She wrote, "This familiar life and body will not come again." And I paused there.

It seemed fairly obvious in writing it—this life and body of which I have grown so fond and with which I have grown so familiar are not permanent. I had an encounter with the stark reality of my own mortality in 2010 when I developed a pulmonary embolism and ended up in the hospital. That experience thrust me into a far more intense appreciation for everything in my life.

A phrase rose up in my heart: "savor *this* life and *this* body." A question began to shimmer for me: What if the meaning of my life is to experience my particular life, my lens on the world, my encounters with grief and loss, delight and joy, but all as my unique story, never to be repeated again? What might I discover by remembering this daily? How might my relationship to my own experience and to this wondrous vessel that carries me through it all be transformed if I not just offer gratitude for my life but savor it with relish, knowing that this moment will never again happen? And to trust that this moment carries profound wisdom, I need to transform my service to the world.

There was so much sweetness that winter after being in the hospital, as I walked hand in hand with my beloved through parks with bare trees, so grateful to be together and alive. I found myself deeply in love with this man, in that moment, and I savored the feel of his rough skin against mine. I savored his gaze over at me, so full of love and familiarity. I savored the way his breath made a faint cloud with each exhale on that chilly evening.

Out of this experience with death came a sense of urgency for me in my life. The things I have wanted to do someday, like live overseas, suddenly became much more important to pay attention to.

What happens when we delay our dreams, when we push aside the subtle whispers that rise up when we are quiet for a while? How do they lose their vigor and insistency through a haze of indifference or holding them off?

Our days are truly jewels, each one a treasure, another opportunity to savor the story emerging in our lives. Even the difficult threads—maybe especially the difficult ones.

The root of the word *savor* comes from the Latin word *saporem*, which means *to taste* and is also the root of *sapient*, which is the word for *wisdom*. Another definition I love is "to give oneself over to the enjoyment of" something. When I give myself over to the experience of savoring, wisdom emerges. Savoring calls for a kind of surrender.

Savoring calls me to slowness (I can't savor quickly), and to spaciousness (I can't savor everything at once), and to mindfulness (I can't savor without being fully present).

It also calls for a fierce and wise discernment about how I spend my time and energy. Now that I know deep in my bones the limits of my life breaths, how do I choose to spend those dazzling hours? What are the experiences ripening within me that long for exploration?

There is also a seasonal quality to savoring—this season, what is right before me, right now, is to be savored. It will rise and fall, come into fullness, and then slip away. When I savor, I pay attention to all the moments of that experience without trying to change it.

Finally, there is a tremendous sweetness to this openhearted way of being in the world. Everything becomes grace because I recognize it could all be different; it could all be gone. Rather than grasp at how I think this moment should be, I savor the way things are.

Surrender to the wisdom of this moment. See what you discover waiting for you right here, right now.

Part One

Listening for a Word

This journey is divided into three parts. The first part is listening for the word, when we learn to drop our need to strive and reach and to let the word come to us as a gift. There are many ways you might do this, and I offer several reflections, meditations, and practices in the pages that follow. There is nothing to achieve here, no quest to embark on, no prize to win—simply a practice of softening our need to make something happen and attune to what is arising in our prayer. We are cultivating our intuitive capacities.

Do not feel like there is a deadline of these first ten days to receive your word. The word may take longer than that to arrive. You can linger for as long as you need in this first set of practices. Trust the process that is unfolding in you. Allowing this unfolding within you, rather than trying to direct things, is a central part of the wisdom of this journey.

1

Cross the Threshold

A threshold is a potent image as we enter a new year or season of life. I love doors and portals and what they represent. While I have mixed feelings about New Year's resolutions, I do adore the promise and possibility this time of year offers us. Doors, both open and closed, seem to shimmer with the invitation to approach.

One of the things I loved most about our time living in central Europe was the beautiful doors to be found in old cities. Doors are places for pausing, of finding your key, of knocking, of asking for entry. Thresholds carry us from one place to another, usually from outside to inside or the other way around. They are symbols of our inner movements.

I believe that our lives are about crossing one threshold after another—opening our hearts to the next invitation, even if it means stepping away from what is comfortable and familiar toward what feels unknown.

When we cross a threshold, we enter a liminal space, which is where the old has been released, dissolved, or sometimes ripped away and the new has not yet taken shape. We often want to grasp the shape of a known future, but this does not honor the richness of our lives and the grace that time can offer as we grow into who we are called to be.

I invite you to pause now and allow some time to rest on whatever threshold you happen to be crossing in this season of your life. See yourself standing in a doorway, straddling the old and the new, but instead of trying to cross over to the other side, you allow time to become familiar with this space of mystery and unknowing. You make space to savor the sacredness of a threshold.

In Ireland, places are referred to as *thin* where the veil between heaven and earth becomes more transparent. These threshold places are ancient sites like holy wells, church ruins, stone circles, passage tombs, and sacred mountains. It is at these thresholds where we become more deeply attuned to the presence of the sacred around us. These places are vessels that can hold us in our times of listening and waiting.

The veil is thought to be thinner at certain times of year, like the solar festivals of the solstices and equinoxes or the Celtic cross-quarter feasts of Samhain, Imbolc, Bealtaine, and Lughnasadh. Samhain is the start of the Celtic new year, so another possibility is to move through these practices in October, leading up to November 1 Samhain.

Ancient wisdom says not all time is the same. Kairos moments, when we have a sense of the holy breaking through, help us to touch eternity and lose track of time, while chronos moments are the tedium of watching the clock tick. Similarly, not all space is the same. Some places are sanctuaries for connection to the sacred, perhaps because of the community of people who have prayed there through the ages.

Whatever threshold you stand on right now, nurture your awareness of how the sacred is more available in these moments, more clearly heard or seen. Keep alert for signs of how the divine is moving through your days.

The world is on a threshold as well. Climate crises, poverty, racism, and violence break our hearts and overwhelm our spirits. When we acknowledge the threshold we are on, we recognize that the old ways must be dissolved and space for the new kept open and alive. When we stand in a doorway, we are listening for ourselves but also listening for those around us who are struggling and suffering in various ways.

You might be inspired by these words from past participants about their own threshold experiences:

> What threshold am I on? Grief. Rage. Despair. Fear of opening up. Becoming conscious of distorted thinking/beliefs that are keeping me stuck. Not knowing if this is the time to move to a different threshold (which parts of me very much want to do but don't know how) or if I need to stay here for a while yet.
>
> What do I need to forgive myself for? Distraction. Contempt. Not applying myself deeply enough. Not seeing.
>
> What is stirring in my heart? Longing. So much longing. To belong, to feel peace, to trust the Divine, to know my purpose. Mostly to have inner peace and presence.
>
> What is my intention/desire for this retreat? To stay connected to myself. To not be in so much emotional pain . . . maybe I should be saying to welcome the pain, to have compassion for the pain, to rest, to feel encircled by the Divine within and without, to be true to myself, pausing to ask, what is really needed in this moment? (Inge Zwikker)

> I am embracing the idea of waiting for the word instead of striving to find the word. I want to wait with an intention to what is happening around me and trust the word will reveal itself and I will know how to carry it with me into the new year. The waiting is so synergistic with advent—there is excitement and anxiety at the same moment. (Paulette Thabault)

Meditation: The Doorway

Take a few slow, deep breaths and center yourself, bringing your awareness from your mind to your heart. Imagine you are dropping down into your body, into the place of receptivity and intuition.

Rest here in the sanctuary of the heart for a few moments, allowing yourself space to simply *be.* Become aware of the presence of the infinite Source of Compassion, who dwells within you like an enduring flame.

As you rest here, begin to open the eyes of your heart to a doorway appearing in front of you. Allow some time to notice how this portal appears to you—the color and texture of it, the shape of it, your felt sense about the door.

Bring a sense of reverence to this door, knowing that it represents a new season of your life beckoning to you.

Reach out your hand and turn the knob. Slowly open the door and stand there at the threshold between the old and the new. Notice how you feel there in this liminal space.

As you dwell on the threshold, become aware of any longings or desires you carry in your heart. What are your hopes for the season ahead? What is the prayer you carry with you? Attune to what the words of the prayer might be for you, holding it lightly, knowing that the journey will reveal its own direction as you move through.

Ask that you receive a word in the coming days, one to nourish and inspire you over many months. Ask that you attune and listen to the ways the word might arrive in your life.

Gently bring your awareness back to the room you are in, and take some time to reflect on what you noticed and discovered.

2

Listen with the Heart

The heart is the primary organ of our physical, emotional, and spiritual well-being. Across religious traditions, mystics consider it to be the dwelling place of God or Spirit. The heart is at the center of our being but also at the center of transcendent realities with which we come into communion through the heart. It is the organ of divine revelation.

Eastern Orthodox theologian and bishop Kallistos Ware describes it this way: "In the innermost depths of my heart I transcend the bounds of my created personhood and discover within myself the direct unmediated presence of the living God. Entry into the deep heart means that I experience myself as God-sourced, God-enfolded, God-transfigured." When I enter into the heart of my being, I recognize myself as having my source in God, being embraced and enfolded by the divine, and being transformed by God.

Saint Benedict begins his rule by inviting us to "listen carefully . . . with the ear of your heart." When he calls us to do this, he means to listen in a way that is different from our ordinary, everyday sense of hearing. Because the heart is our intimate connection to the sacred presence and where our transfiguration takes place, it is the organ for listening to the sacred shimmering through words and our lives.

Because of the world we live in and what it values and upholds, we tend to listen most often from the ego or the mind. We listen to understand, to figure out, to make plans, to see what we can exploit. This kind of listening is transactional.

The heart is an axial point, a center of unity within the person as a whole. It is an ancient metaphor for the seat of our whole being—to be wholehearted means to bring our entire selves before God: our intellect, our emotional life, our dreams and intuitions, our deepest longings. The heart is both a physical reality of a necessary organ pumping blood in our chest throughout our system and a spiritual symbol of integration and union with the divine. It is the place that knows and understands who we truly are, beneath the compulsions and distractions, beyond the false idols and personas we create. The thinking mind will try to control what unfolds or analyze and judge the process.

The heart is where we find the Source of Compassion with us, an endless fountain of love and care where we know ourselves as intimately intertwined with other human beings and all of creation. When we listen with the heart, we invite God to speak to us without mediation. We attune to the sensations in our body, the images that arise, the feelings we have. It is the deepest core of who we are and the organ of capacity for God's intimate presence with us. The heart is the place of meaning-making, where we discover how we are called to be in the world.

Meditation: Heart-Centered Practice

I invite you into a very simple heart-centered practice to cultivate this posture of listening. Begin by becoming aware of your body. Notice how your body is feeling by simply being present to sensations you are experiencing. Welcome in both the body's delight and the body's discomfort. Notice if there are any areas holding tension and see if you can soften into those places.

Connect to your breath, deepening it gently. As you inhale, imagine the Breath of Life breathing into you. As you exhale, allow yourself to experience a moment of release and surrender to this time and place, becoming fully present. Take a couple of cycles of breath to simply notice this life-sustaining rhythm, which continues moment by moment even when you are unaware of it.

In your imagination, gently allow your breath to carry your awareness from your head (which is your thinking, analyzing, judging center) down to your heart center (where you experience life from a place of greater integration, feeling, and intuition). This movement is not forced but more of an allowing.

Imagine your heart as a great magnetic force drawing your attention into your center.

Consider placing your hand on your heart to experience a physical connection with your heart center and draw your awareness to this place. Rest in this heart-centered space for a while. Release expectations of what the experience will be, staying open to the surprising ways of God.

Breathe into your heart center and begin to simply notice what you are feeling right now in this moment without judging or trying to change it. Allow your breath to soften this space around your heart. Take a few moments to be present with whatever it is you are feeling and make some room within yourself to experience this without pushing it away. Welcome in the full spectrum of who you are, whether grief, anger, boredom, joy, anxiety, serenity.

Taking another breath, call to mind the spark of God, which the ancient monks and mystics tell us dwells in your heart. Bring the infinite compassion of God to however you are feeling right now, not trying to change anything but just gently holding yourself in this space.

As you experience yourself filling with compassion for your own experience, imagine breathing that compassion out into the world and connecting to other hearts—both human and animal—beating across the world in a rhythm of love. Allow that love to expand within you with each inhale, and as you exhale, imagine allowing it to expand into the space around you, getting wider with each breath.

Allow a few moments of silence to simply listen from this heart-centered space. What do you notice from this awareness? Is there anything about your attention that has shifted?

Let your heart fill with gratitude for whatever your experience has been and for the gift of a holy pause in which to simply rest in what is.

3

Let the Word Choose You

When we bring this desire for a life-giving word to be spoken to us for the year or season ahead, we might be tempted to think our way into the word, to analyze what would be the best, most efficient, and practical word possible. But it doesn't work like this. We can't think our way into this journey.

Rather than choosing a word, I invite you to *let a word choose you.* What does this mean exactly? How am I chosen by a word? It means releasing your thinking mind and expectations and resting into your heart. If you are thinking of New Year's resolutions and which word would be most motivating for you to lose those last ten pounds, this is not what we're talking about. It means softening your grasp and letting go of the reaching. It means surrendering into a place of deep trust and receptivity.

When I teach about contemplative photography, I describe the difference between "taking" photos and "receiving" them. So much of our language is about taking, whether we refer to photos, or taking time, or taking advantage, or other things in our lives. Photography also uses such aggressive terms as *shooting* and *capturing*. It reflects a cultural mindset where we go out into the world looking for what we want and seizing it.

When we receive photos, or gifts, or words, we enter into a different kind of presence to the world—one that is less expectant of an outcome and more in wonder at holy surprise. We move through our lives often grasping at things, but this kind of practice asks us to breathe deeply and soften our grip, let our palms open, and walk through the world with a sense of gratitude at what comes.

What if I trusted that a word would come when the time was ripe? What if I let go of the need to find something for myself and opened myself to receive what comes? If you find yourself obsessing over the "right" word, it is time to breathe and let go. Pay attention to synchronicities around you. Look for images that shimmer and make your heart stir with delight. Notice what is making you uncomfortable, calling you to grow beyond the known edges of your life. These are the places where your word will make itself known. Eventually.

For some of you, the word may come right away, but others may find the process much slower. Trust that perhaps it is the waiting itself that is being offered to you as wisdom and practice. The word comes as a gift. You will often know it through an intuitive experience, a more embodied sense of *yes*. The word (or phrase) is one that will *work in you* (rather than you working on it). Remember that a word that creates a sense of inner resistance is as important to pay attention to as one that has a great deal of resonance.

Meditation: Breath Prayer

When you awaken in the morning, try practicing a simple breath prayer while holding your hands outstretched, palms open and facing upward. It can be helpful to begin by grasping your hands into a fist as tightly as you can, and then on a long, slow exhale, let your fingers soften and open.

Breath prayer is a very simple practice of aligning a word or phrase with our inhale and exhale. You can pray with any words at all, but I am suggesting how this particular prayer may begin.

As you breathe in, softly say the words *I wait* to yourself. This is not the kind of waiting we do in line at the post office or bank but a more attentive waiting where we are waiting on the Holy One to shimmer in some way.

As you breathe out, say the words *to receive* to yourself. Let your hands open even wider in a posture of welcome. Again, this is not like receiving a paycheck or a phone call but the reception of an unexpected gift.

Breathe in: *I wait*
Breathe out: *to receive*

Let yourself steep in this prayer for five minutes. When you find yourself striving or reaching for something, let your breath soften your grip and return to this posture of openness and attending.

4

Listen to Your Life

Lectio divina is one of the primary practices in the Christian monastic tradition for listening for a word or phrase that shimmers or calls to our hearts. *Lectio* is traditionally applied to Scripture but can also be engaged to pray with other sacred texts, such as our life experience. *Lectio divina* offers us a widened capacity for awareness that God dwells in each moment.

The practice of *lectio* invites us to consider how we might read each moment as shimmering with sacred presence. We are each words of God; each page of our lives reveals something of the holy. We don't often see the sacred within because we are so distracted. We live with dulled vision, so we only see life's surfaces—the demands and anxieties and struggles of daily living—or we numb ourselves to the pain with distractions, deafening our ears to the call to rest in silence and listen.

We constantly tell the stories of our lives. Sometimes the story we tell, however, keeps us stuck in certain patterns of expectation. We can outgrow who we understood ourselves to be. Stories can be empowering but also limiting. The invitation to pray with our lives is not about reaffirming what we already know about ourselves but entering into prayer in an openhearted way to receive the grace and new vision offered to us. We pray with our lives as sacred texts to reveal new places of freedom, invitations to new ways of understanding ourselves, and the ways God is moving through our stories.

Meditation: *Lectio Divina* with Life Experience

Allow some time to settle into your chair and sink into your body. Become aware of your breathing, gently deepening it. As you inhale, imagine the breath of God filling not just your body but the whole of your life with enlivening energy. As you exhale, imagine letting go of whatever keeps you from being fully present in your life.

Allow your breath to carry your awareness down to your heart center. Rest in this space for a few moments, perhaps resting your hand over your heart and relishing the rhythm of your heartbeat, which sustains your life.

Spend some time with your imagination reviewing this last year, honoring it as a sacred text. Begin to "read" your experience. In your imagination, walk through this past year, noticing where your attention is being drawn, welcoming in whichever memories or feelings arise. Move through the year in an openhearted and spacious way and notice if there is a particular moment that deserves some more attention. Listen for how your heart is being led. Make room within you to allow this moment to unfold in your imagination. Savor the sense experience of it. What do you remember of sight, smell, taste, touch, and sound? Are there images, colors, or symbols rising up into your awareness? Be present to the feelings that are being stirred and welcome them in.

Notice if there is a word or phrase that rises up (this may not be *the word*, so release the pressure). Then allow that word to unfold in your imagination and welcome in images, feelings, and memories that stir in you.

After a time of making space for these, begin to ask: What is the invitation or call rising up from these noticings? Where is God calling you to a new awareness or action in your life? Do you sense how you are being called in your life to respond to this moment? Which action or awareness is emerging from your reflection on this time?

Close with a period of silence. Gently release everything that has been stirring in you. Connect to your breath again and allow the rhythm of your breath to fill you with peace, letting go of words and images so you can rest fully into a few moments of contemplative presence. Give yourself some time simply to be, remembering that your life is about more than the sum of your experiences and what you do in the world. Then release even this awareness and come to a place of deep stillness.

When you are ready to complete this time of prayer, allow your breath to bring your awareness gently back to the outer space of your room. Take some time to journal about what emerged in your prayer experience, writing about any moment that called for more attention.

Feel free to repeat this meditation as often as needed and notice which life experiences rise up to the surface.

Here are words from past participants about what was revealed to them during this meditation:

> The words that jumped out to me in this meditation were "release that pressure," and I felt my body relax. I am eager to get on to the next thing and have a word in my pocket ready to go, but this encouragement today was to ease into it and release the pressure to perform and produce that I put on myself.

So, holding my impatience in check, I will release the pressure and wait. (Sarah Pickering)

When I saw the title of today's session, I admittedly recoiled at the thought of having to read . . . as even that small act seems to surpass my energy reserves at the moment. How soon I was surprised to learn that we can also . . . read our own lives. How counterintuitive. Or is it? I know our lives can be a prayer, so why not also a book of sorts? At the end of it all, is a story not all that's left? The growth is in disentangling ourselves from our own narratives while also being enriched by them. It brought me back to basics as well . . . with Jesus himself being the Word. (Bridget O'Grady)

What wisdom is revealed to you?

5

Reflect on What Has Been Life-Giving and Life-Draining

The Examen prayer was created by Ignatius of Loyola, a sixteenth-century Spanish mystic, and he recommended praying it at the end of each day, reflecting on what has been most life-giving and life-draining. It is a prayerful way of reflecting on the movements of the divine in our lives, similar to *lectio divina* but with a different focus. When we practice it daily, we can start to notice patterns of consolation and desolation in our lives, which offer wisdom for how we are to live.

We can adapt this prayer practice as a reflection on the past year. I offer a version of it below to pray it in this way, and I invite you into gentle arm movements as a way of attuning to the wisdom of the body as well. If you have any physical limitations or prefer to pray this in stillness, please feel free to adapt as needed.

Meditation: Embodied Examen

Begin by finding a comfortable position and moving your attention inward. Draw your attention to your body with your breath. Deepen your breathing and, with each inhale, imagine you are welcoming in the life breath of God, who sustains you moment by moment. With each exhale, imagine you are releasing whatever is keeping you from being fully present. Take a few breaths, paying attention to this rhythm of breathing in the life force, breathing out what is distracting.

Reach both of your arms down.

Become aware of your connection to the earth and its support beneath you. Feel it beneath you. Imagine you are sending roots down through your arms and legs and drawing up nourishment from the earth.

What do you need to ground you and bring your awareness to the present moment?

Which concerns keep you from being fully here? Can you allow God to hold them for this time?

What is awakening beneath the ground of your being?

Breathe and just notice what stirs in you, making space for it.

Reach back behind you with your right arm.

Begin to move through this last year in your imagination. As you look back on this last year, ask yourself: What were the most life-giving experiences for you? Where did you feel most filled with love? Hope? Just notice which moments come to mind and stay with them. Then choose just one to enter into. Take a few moments to experience this in your body. How does revisiting this moment feel for you? Where do you experience a quickening?

Is there anyone you want to thank for this memory? Spend a few moments dwelling in gratitude.

Take a deep breath and exhale, releasing your arm.

Reach back behind you with your left arm.

Again, reflecting on this last year, ask yourself: What were the most life-draining experiences for you? Where did you feel most restless? The least hopeful? Notice which moments come to mind and stay with them without judgment or trying to change them. Then choose just one to enter into. How does revisiting this moment feel for you in your body? Where do you experience it? Take a few moments to be with this.

Is there anyone you want to offer forgiveness for this experience? Spend a few moments seeing if you are moved to extend forgiveness, including to yourself.

Take another deep breath and exhale, releasing your arm.

Reach both of your arms forward.

Holding a heart of gratitude and forgiveness, how do you want to move forward into the year ahead?

What are your hopes? How are you being invited to follow the Spirit now?

How do you nurture the new seeds of life being stirred within you?

What do you notice in your body?

Reach both of your arms upward.

What is the guidance you need to support you in any of these needs?

What do you want to ask for to help you move more fully into your hopes for the day?

How might you call on God for this guidance?

Reach inward and bring your hands to prayer position or leave them open to your sides in a receiving posture.

What new things do you notice now stirring within you?

What is awakening within you?

Which desires and insights invite further reflection?

Which new questions do you bring to your discernment process?

Gently bring your awareness back to the room and spend some time in reflection, writing about your experience and noticing the inner movements that happened. Were there any words that shimmered for you? Hold this lightly.

6

Give Me One Wild Word

In her book *Finding Beauty in a Broken World*, Terry Tempest Williams describes going out to the rocky shore in Maine at dusk and asking the sea, "Give me one wild word." I love this image of a "wild word," a word that moves us past our preconceived ideas and expectations.

The natural world can be a powerful place to discover the divine presence shimmering forth. I invite you on a contemplative walk, which is a walk where you aren't trying to get anywhere. Your sole purpose is to be as present as possible to each footfall. If you have mobility issues, you can do a contemplative walk looking out your window or in the reflective space of your imagination.

Listen for how your inner life is calling you forward with each step. Be present to the gifts of creation around you (even if it is the city pigeons and trees planted down the sidewalk). Listen if they might have a word to offer you.

Ask the birds, the creatures, the stones, the leaves and flowers, the wind for a "wild word," which is a word that calls you to a place of greater freedom.

You can let this walk be enough, or if you feel inspired to create, you might also follow the invitation below to gather materials for a nature mandala.

Meditation: Creating a Nature Mandala

As you walk, you might want to experiment with some spontaneous art-making along the way. Become aware of materials along your path that could be used for your own creation—stones, sticks, leaves, flowers. See if you can use found materials rather than breaking off branches or stems. The earth offers up plenty of organic material to the great compost of life.

Let this be a contemplative experience, listening for which objects shimmer for you, what seems to hold wisdom or meaning or stories.

Once you have gathered enough materials, find a place to pause and enter into a time of creation. Arrange leaves into a mandala, create a nature altar, or whatever form of expression you most desire to enter into.

Release the thinking, judging mind as much as possible. When thoughts do enter in, simply notice them, then let them go and return to your task. Let your creative process flow like a river until it arrives where it is going.

Ask the stones where they want to be laid; have a conversation with the twigs and leaves about how they want to be in relationship to one another. If the whole idea of talking to your materials makes you feel foolish, embrace the foolishness and remember that this is about prayer and play and taking yourself less seriously.

When you have arrived at your "destination" and have a feeling of satisfaction with what has been created, simply sit with it for a while. Just notice your own experience. What do you discover as a creator? How do you experience this kind of cocreation with the natural world?

You might want to receive this creation with a photo. Or you might not. Check in to see whether a photo feels too grasping, too much like checking off an assignment or trying to create something permanent rather than allowing yourself an experience. Trust whatever emerges in response. Thank the materials for their invitation to you to participate with them in creating more beauty. Listen for a "wild word" that might be offered.

Then walk away. Practice humility and surrender by knowing that the organic nature of things means that this creation will eventually disintegrate back to the earth rather than be forever captured in the great halls of a museum. Like the Buddhist monks who create intricate mandalas from colored sand and then blow all the sand away, see if you can practice nonattachment and be compassionate with any resistance you experience, just noticing it as good food for reflection.

7

Tend the Night Wisdom of Dreams

In ancient times, dreams were respected as signs from God, invitations to a calling bigger than we might imagine in our waking life and the limits of daylight vision. Dreams can be vital to pay attention to during times of discernment as they give clues and indications of the soul's unique gifts and longings. They can help to support us in our *yes* to a life that is uniquely our own, to say yes to the gifts that can only be birthed through us.

Dreams play a significant role in Scripture, with guidance and direction often arriving in these night visions. From Joseph of the Old Testament and Jacob's dream of a staircase from earth to heaven with angels ascending and descending, to Daniel's dream of the four beasts and Joseph of the New Testament having four separate dreams that are recalled in the Gospels: in the first he is told not to be afraid to take pregnant Mary as his wife; Joseph is then warned in a second dream to leave Bethlehem and flee to Egypt; while in Egypt, Joseph has a third dream where he is told that it is safe to go back to Israel; and in the fourth dream, he is warned to avoid Judea, so he departed for the region of Galilee. God regularly appears to people through such means, offering important messages.

Dreams call us into a way of being that is less linear and more intuitive, less goal-driven and more open to receiving the gifts being offered to us in the moment. Our own dreams may seem much less straightforward than these biblical and saintly dreams. They speak a language that can feel confusing to our waking mind, so we must approach them with reverence and hospitality. There is a grace offered in listening to their wisdom.

Practice: Working with Dreams

If you usually can't remember your dreams, one of the best ways to invite memory is to place a journal and a pen by your bed at night before sleep and then ask God for a dream. Even if you awaken with only a fragment or a feeling, record that on waking. Honor whatever comes and be aware when you dismiss dream images because you think they are too mundane or strange.

You might even ask explicitly for a word to be revealed through night wisdom and see what happens, accepting if your dreams seem silent on the matter.

Consider strong dream images as possible words calling to you. Pay attention to synchronicities that follow from dreams throughout the day. Are there images or words that seem to repeat themselves? If so, take note.

I find it most helpful to write down the dream in present tense, so as not to distance oneself from it, and give it a title. Each of the characters or symbols that appear represents an aspect of yourself. Often, the more fearful elements of a dream are part of our shadow selves, which have not yet been integrated.

It can also help to write down the dream in symbols or visual language, so, as you write out the narrative, when you come to something that could be depicted in a simple symbol, draw that instead of the word. Another helpful tool is not necessarily writing your dream from left to right in a linear way, as we do in journaling. Write the dream in a spiral, or sideways in your notebook, or upside down on the page. This signals to the mind that we are not working with linear ways.

Choose one character or dream symbol to begin. Write from the perspective of this image. Begin with "I am" and speak from the voice of this energy. How does it experience the world? What is it like to see through this particular lens?

After you have written for a while, the next step is to embody the dream character. Take a few moments to center yourself and connect with your breath, bring this energy into your body and see how it feels. How does this character or symbol move through the world? What gestures or postures might it take? Explore the different physical possibilities for several minutes.

Try this for several dream symbols and then enter them into a dialogue with one another, either on paper through writing or by moving back and forth physically between the embodied energies. Notice what you discover. Ask the dream symbols for a word and see what is offered.

When we descend into the holy darkness of night and receive an invitation through symbol and imagery, we are called to trust in the imagination of a God much bigger than ourselves.

Despite these efforts at readying yourself to receive a dream, if you are still unable to remember any on awakening, you can tap into the wisdom of the liminal time on awakening. At the threshold of morning, we are still in the dreamtime state, and even if we can't remember specific images, we can bring ourselves present to what we are feeling.

Keep a journal by your bed and every morning when you wake, make a commitment to write for 10–15 minutes without editing or stopping whatever comes to mind. It may be a particular dream that you had, or it may be just a feeling or image you are aware of. Some mornings may feel cloudy with confusion; you can write about that. Do this writing exploration before you check your email or social media and before you talk to anyone else. You want to dwell in that in-between space between sleep and wakefulness and honor whatever you notice there. These little tidbits may seem meaningless some mornings, and some days you may start to see patterns and new insights being revealed. This practice is valuable even if you do not remember your dreams.

Another way you might do this practice is to look up an online oracle. You can do an online search for these. Here are two examples: https://dianacooper.com/pick-a-card/ and https://www.alanafairchild.com/online-oracle/.

You might have a deck of cards at home as well. These can generate a lovely sense of serendipity and synchronicity, where a word or image lands in your life somewhat like a dream. Prayerfully choose a card for guidance and then, whatever word arrives, work with it like a dream. See if it has anything to say about your life right now.

8

Consult a Soul Friend

A key to the desert and Celtic contemplative traditions was having a soul friend. The desert elders were sought out by thousands, desiring a deeper life of faith, seeking wisdom that comes from life experience. Patrick and Brigid both express how vital this was for their lives. Saint Brigid is often quoted as saying, "Go forth and eat nothing until you get a soul friend, for anyone without a soul friend is like a body without a head; it is like the water of a polluted lake, neither good for drinking nor for washing. That is the person without a soul friend."

Everyone, whether layperson or clergy, regardless of gender, was expected to have a spiritual mentor and companion on the soul's journey. This was a person with whom you could confide all of your inner struggles, someone who would help you find your path and could midwife you in discernment. This relationship came with a sense of genuine warmth and intimacy, as well as deep respect for the other's wisdom as a source of blessing. Age or gender differences did not matter.

There should not be a wandering from one soul friend to another, or else there is the danger of only a superficial relationship. Full honesty and truthfulness were expected. The tradition of a soul friend reinforces the communal and corporate nature of desert and Celtic spirituality and the dangers of traveling the spiritual path alone.

A soul friend helps to offer us the courage needed to say yes to the big dreams being birthed in us. They help us to gain clarity over places of self-deception and denial.

It is said that Patrick used to have an angel who visited him regularly named Victor. He offered Patrick his guidance, sometimes in dreams. Victor was a kind of guardian spirit. Soul friends can be those who have passed through the veil and continue to offer us support and wisdom.

Esther De Waal, in her book *The Celtic Way of Prayer: The Recovery of the Religious Imagination*, writes, "The relationship of soul-friendship existed between men and women, women and women, men and men, cleric and lay. The soul-friend was the spiritual guide who helped everyone to find his or her own path. The practice of seeing one's soul-friend on a regular basis seems to have been expected by all who committed themselves to the relationship."

I invite you to seek out a soul friend. You may already have one in your life, a spiritual director, a wise guide, someone you can turn to when things feel challenging to entrust the secrets of your heart. Honesty with all of the inner grumbling gives it space to dissipate under the gaze of mindful and compassionate attention.

Sometimes seeking out a professional is the best way forward. There are many ways to find a spiritual direction or companion, and a fee helps to create a fair exchange of energy. Spiritual directors are trained to hold space for whatever it is you bring around your spiritual journey. They can also refer you to a psychotherapist, if needed.

A soul friend acts as a witness, someone who affirms where we are and can offer counsel when we want to run far away. This is why the spiritual journey is always done in community, because the shadow parts of ourselves we explored can fool us into actions that aren't the best for us.

Practice: Cultivating Soul Friendship

I feel fortunate to have had different kinds of soul friends in my life. Certainly, John, as my beloved spouse, is also the person in my life with whom I am most intimate. He knows most of my failings as well as my gifts. In so many ways, his love for me has healed many long-standing wounds from childhood. The places in our lives where we conflict are just as valuable as the places where we come together in unison. It is a gift to witness his life's unfolding alongside my own and see how they might weave together.

I also have a spiritual director who takes on that more formal role and whom I meet with regularly. As someone who does this kind of work with others, I find it essential to have someone who can hold space for my process. I began to see him a couple of years after my mother died. I was struggling deeply at that time with depression and what I later came to recognize as a dark night of the soul. My image of God was being broken apart, and this person accompanied me on the slow path to embracing a wider one. When I moved overseas, I first assumed I would go on to find a new spiritual director in my new home country. But after we moved from Seattle to Vienna, everything and everyone was so new, and I was so hungry for people in my life who already knew my story. So I was grateful to be able to continue our connection by Skype and then Zoom, a relationship that endures now that I live in Ireland, and I love that he has known my journey for these many years and can help illuminate patterns and reveal shadow places. He has been a wise guide in my life for more than ten years now, for which I am deeply grateful.

I also have several very dear and close women friends whom I would consider soul friends in my life. They are women with whom I share regular conversations about the goings-on of life and who always reach down beneath the superficial layers and into the matters of the heart. These are women who know me well and help support and challenge me.

I have also been blessed many times in my life with animals who have acted as soul friends. I am a dog person through and through, and I cherish how my connection to animal wisdom deepens my own path. While we were living in Sacramento, the Bay Area, and Seattle, our dogs were long-term members of the family. When we first adopted Tune, an eight-year-old Weimaraner who had spent her life in a breeding kennel utterly neglected, her gratitude for a new life was palpable. She bonded to us immediately, even as she continued to be wary of other people. In her four years with us, she taught me much about healing the wounds of the heart, about slow rhythms, and about unconditional love.

Finally, I have also found, much like Saint Patrick, that my ancestors and others who have passed through the veil can continue to act as soul friends. Certainly, the witness of people like Saint Hildegard of Bingen and Saint Benedict of Nursia continues to nourish and challenge my path. Time and space are not limits on this relationship.

Reflect on someone in your life who knows you very well—a partner, a dear friend, a spiritual director, a wise elder, an ancestor, or a creature in your life—and approach them to ask for a word. The word might be a phrase and is something you can reflect on for many months to come. They might need some time to ponder this with you.

One of our retreat participants, Carolyn Bowers, shares the ways she has been enriched and challenged by her spiritual director:

> "I have had the same spiritual director since October 2007. It has been a rich relationship that has grown through the years and held me through many changing circumstances. When I ask my spiritual director for a word, she gave me 'Be still and know.' This helped confirm the word(s) that I am hearing: Wait, Trust, Do not be afraid. I feel I am being called into a season of openness and patience, trusting that God has me in hand through whatever comes along. These are not easy things for me."

9

Read a Set of Wisdom Principles

I invite you to turn to a set of spiritual principles for some wisdom or guidance. These might be the texts of an established wisdom tradition or can be from a more modern set of guidelines. Consider either choosing something you are already deeply familiar with and reading with fresh eyes or choosing something far from your life experience that might break you open in new ways.

Here are some suggestions (you can do an online search for these to read about them in more depth):

- The Beatitudes in Matthew's Gospel (5:3–12)
- Micah 6:8 (What does God require of you but to do justice and to love kindness and to walk humbly with your God?)

- The Ten Commandments (Exodus 20:1–17), which form a core set of ethical guidance for the Jewish and Christian traditions
- The Eightfold Noble Path, which is central to Buddhist practice
- The five niyamas of yoga: *saucha* (cleanliness), *santosha* (contentment), *tapas* (fire of discipline), *svadhyaya* (study of the self and of the texts), *ishvara pranidhana* (surrender to a higher power)
- The 12 Steps of Alcoholics Anonymous
- Do an online search for Mary Oliver's poem "In Blackwater Woods" and pray with the three things she says we must be able to do
- At our community, Abbey of the Arts, we have a set of principles we call the Monk Manifesto (https://abbeyofthearts.com/about/monk-manifesto/), which is meant to be a source of support for contemplative living and integrated wisdom from several streams

Meditation: *Lectio Divina*

Choose which set of principles you want to pray with and reflect on, and engage in the practice of *lectio divina* with the text, which is a slow and contemplative reading. We are not reading for information but for transformation. Release any reaching or grasping you might notice as you desire to have your word find you. Let this practice simply be an opportunity to rest in the arms of the Beloved.

Allow a few moments to center yourself and drop your awareness from your mind into your heart. Rest in the sanctuary of the heart, allowing time to simply *be*. Release your doing for several breaths. Become aware of the Source of Love pulsing here within you.

Slowly read the text you have chosen, in a contemplative way. Listen for the places where your heart shimmers and those where you pull back. Notice your inner response to these invitations, these principles to live by. Both resonance and resistance can be helpful to pay attention to.

Once a word for this prayer practice has arrived, sit with it and let it echo in your heart. You might speak it aloud to see how it feels in your mouth or sounds around you. You might try singing or chanting it aloud and experience the vibration of it in your body and in the room.

Let images, memories, and feelings unfold from this word. Allow the prayer to arise organically, no need to force anything; simply pay attention to the resonances that come. Make a welcoming space in your heart for all of this to flow. Try to release any judgment of images that may arise. Trust that the process of prayer is leading you to deeper wisdom.

Then listen for any sense of invitation that might emerge from this time of prayer. How is the divine calling you to a new awareness in your life? Might this word or phrase be one that speaks to your heart for the year ahead? How does it call or challenge you? Do you feel a longing to deepen into its invitation in the coming weeks and months? Is it something you could see yourself living with for the seasons ahead and gaining more fruit over time? How does it spark a sense of deeper love in your heart?

Once you have received the invitation, rest in silence for a few minutes, letting go of words and images. Settle into the stillness, simply basking in gratitude for whatever has come. Be in the presence of the sacred source of silence.

Gently bring your awareness back to the room and allow some time to journal and reflect.

Read from past participants about their experience with this meditation:

> Reading the Monk Manifesto, the line that jumped out at me was "I commit to a lifetime of ongoing conversion and transformation." The word *conversion* shimmered for me. I don't know if it will become

my word, but I believe that whatever word claims me will need to include the idea of conversion, of change and transformation. It reminds me of *metanoia*, changing course or direction, and I think of many areas of my life that have changed course or could benefit from a new direction. Something to chew on. (Brenda Anderson)

I chose the poetry of Mary Oliver. I tend to gravitate toward enunciated steps and then not follow through. So I chose the poem and it directly spoke to my current reality of having chosen a retirement date. I have ambivalence about retirement. I need intensity in my life and the work of the past 8 years has given that to me along with the knowledge that every day I was making a difference in the lives of people living on the edge. That same intensity takes a toll on my body and soul, especially now in my mid-60s. I was invited by the poem to observe this process of letting go and not knowing in nature and consequently the pattern in all of life today. (Jane Lippert)

The Beatitudes led to the Corporal and Spiritual Works of Mercy. Words are multiplying! Hungry, comfort. Permeate, infiltrate, synergy. Return, conserve, transform, remake, renewal. It's like I put a thesaurus in the blender! (Cynthia Wright)

10

Imagine Your Deathbed

One of the core practices of the ancient monks was to remember their mortality. Saint Benedict wrote, "Keep death daily before one's eyes," and we find this invitation in many of the stories of the ancient monks.

Death of any kind is rarely a welcome experience. Even when we witness the mysteries of nature, year after year, reveal the glories of springtime, which emerge from winter's fallow landscape, we resist death; we try to numb ourselves to life's inevitable stripping away of our "secure" frameworks. We spend so much energy and money on staying young. But when we turn to face death wide-eyed and fully present, when we feel the fullness of the grief it brings, we also slowly begin to discover the new life awaiting us. Many of the desert elders repeated this core teaching of death as a wisdom guide and principle to keep before us daily: "[Amma Sarah] also said, 'I put my foot out to ascend the ladder, and I place death before my eyes before going up it'" (Sarah 6).

Being mindful of our eventual death need not be morbid but calls us to always return to that which is essential. Abba Evagrius, another of the desert elders, calls us to sit in our cell, which is the place of our interior reflection and contemplation. In this sanctuary of the heart, we are invited to imagine the day of our death and discover how this awareness calls us to release that which does not serve us or is not life-giving: "Abba Evagrius said, 'Sit in your cell, collecting your thoughts. Remember the day of your death. See then what the death of your body will be; let your spirit be heavy, take pains, condemn the vanity of the world, so as to be able always to live in the peace you have in view without weakening'" (Evagrius 1).

In his book *Soul Making*, Alan Jones describes the desert relationship to death in this way: "Facing death gives our loving force, clarity, and focus . . . even our despair is to be given up and seen as the ego-grasping device that it really is. Despair about ourselves and our world is, perhaps, the ego's last and, therefore, greatest attachment."

Facing the reality of our death has to do with stripping away our illusions and attachments and remembering the fragile beauty of existence and daily living.

We let go of self-deception and self-destructive behaviors that are based on a sense that we will never die. Acknowledging our death might thrust us into despair, into a sense of life's ultimate futility. Or it might usher us into the reality that there are possibilities far beyond our own imaginings.

In the desert tradition, death is a friend and companion along the journey. Saint Francis of Assisi referred to death as "sister" in his famous poem "Canticle of Creation." Rather than the presence at the end of our lives, death can become a companion along each step, heightening our awareness of life's beauty and calling us toward living more fully. Living with Sister Death calls us to greater freedom and responsibility.

It is precisely in the place of our profound vulnerability as human beings that we can have an encounter with what is most precious in our lives. It can call us to clarity about where we want to direct our attention and care.

Meditation: *Memento Mori*

The purpose of this contemplation is to remember our humanity with humility, to know ourselves as earthy and vulnerable, to know we are not invincible. And out of that tenderness, to remember the treasures of our days and offer gratitude for the gift of another day of being alive.

Allow some time to slow down your breathing and quiet your mind. Let your awareness drop into the sanctuary of your heart. Spend a few moments there breathing with the Holy One, who sustains you day by day. Know there is nothing you need to *do* but let yourself simply *be*.

Invite in the presence of a wise guide, perhaps one of the desert elders or Saint Benedict or another person you feel drawn to for companionship. Ask them to show you lying on your deathbed, soon before your time of crossing the final threshold of this life.

Spend some time entering the scene, feeling the support of your guide, seeing what other companions are there with you.

As you rest there, reflect on your life. What were the regrets? Can you bring compassion and forgiveness? What were the joys? Can you bring gratitude?

Let your life scroll before you like a movie, noticing the challenges and celebrations, the quiet moments, and the times of grief.

Ask yourself, If I were to die today, what would I miss the most from my life? What do I wish I still had time to experience? What feels essential from this perspective?

Notice if there is any word or phrase that arises without trying to grasp or make something happen. Just notice. Rest here for a while and listen.

When you are ready to return, allow a few deep breaths as you gently bring your awareness back to the room. Allow some time to journal about what you noticed or discovered.

While this meditation may seem daunting or frightening at first, be encouraged by this reflection from a past participant:

> The meditation exercise to "imagine your deathbed" is a powerful way to connect with overall life themes and deeper meanings that emerge as a result of such reviews.
>
> This particular contemplation led me to realize I had spent the better part of my life striving for external validation, with all its attendant stresses, rather than gifting myself with self-affirmation. In the past fourteen years of my widowhood, I have learned to listen to and value my own voice, and to offer myself compassion and acceptance for both my gifts and frailties. I am thankful for what I have and what I can offer, including my poetry. I am more focussed now on being, and on entering fully into the blessings of each day, in the realization of how precious and fragile life is.
>
> If I were to die today, I would miss most the people I love, and the opportunities to continue to

experience more of our beautiful earth in all its seasons and places.

The word that surfaced in this exercise has been *connections.* That includes a deeper connection with oneself—the world within—as well as the world without, and fits with my chosen word, *accept*, with a deep resonance. (Anne MacDermaid)

Interlude

Surplus

Surplus was my word for 2017. A couple of summers prior, I had been pondering quite a bit how to make the work I love so much sustainable energetically. Even with work that arises out of passion, we bump up against our limits of what we can give and how much renewal we need. As a contemplative and strong introvert, I have high needs for quiet times, and I am grateful for our seasonal rhythms, which allow for extended times of restoration.

Then the previous summer, my pondering shifted to consider something even more generous than merely sustainable: surplus. I am not just thinking about how to have enough energy and resources to meet the needs of this flourishing community but to have more than enough, a surplus, an excess of reserves.

My word was inspired by a quote I read a couple of years ago by Jungian analyst Robert Johnson in his book *The Fisher King and the Handless Maiden*, where he described how the protagonist of the story goes into the forest for seven years: "Nothing happens, which is enough to frighten any modern person. But that kind of nothingness is the accumulation or storing of healing energy . . . to have a store of energy accumulated is to have power in back of one. We live with our psychic energy in modern times much as we do with our money—mortgaged into the next decade. Most modern people are exhausted nearly all the time and never catch up to an equilibrium of energy, let alone have a store of energy behind them. With no energy in store, one cannot meet any new opportunity."

Those words have stayed with me ever since I read them because I have recognized the call of the monk in them. What makes the monastic path so countercultural is the active resistance against living a life of busyness and exhaustion, of not making that a badge of pride, of having an abundance of time to ponder and live life more slowly and attentively.

How many of us feel our energy is mortgaged into the next decade? How many of us can never catch up with the rest we so desperately need, much less feel like we have a "store of energy" behind us?

There are, of course, seasons of life that sometimes demand more from us energetically. It had been several years since John and I embarked on our life pilgrimage, which uprooted us from our longtime beloved home in Seattle and sent us to Vienna, Austria, for six months and then on to Galway, Ireland, where we finally settled. So much moving and transition over time demanded a lot of inner resources.

I was deepening into this new season of life, not one marked by so much change and wandering but one committed to stability for the long season ahead. One where I fall back in love with the sacred ordinary details of daily life: cherishing old and new friendships, shopping at the market and cooking for nourishment, celebrating the vibrant creative community we have here, enjoying long walks along Galway Bay and noticing something new each time, showing up to my computer each day to write from my heart, swimming, dancing, swooning over life's moments.

Surplus was inviting me into a deep kind of trust that there would be enough—more than enough—time, money, love.

Part Two

Receiving the Word

Has a word emerged yet in your prayer? If not, take heart. Despite this being a thirty-day journey, there is no rush to arrive. You can take all the time you need. This in itself is an essential practice. Allow slowness to be your guide. Return to the practices of the first ten days, especially any that seemed particularly fruitful for you. These practices are rich and can be repeated often with new layers of discovery offered. You can also give yourself a day or two when you release any need to practice and simply listen to the silence to see what emerges in that space.

Repetition of prayer was a key practice for Ignatius of Loyola, a Spanish mystic who created the thirty-day spiritual exercises. It is a time of returning to a previous prayer period and allowing the movements of the divine to deepen. When we repeat our prayers, we attune more deeply to the sacred shimmering through our lives. It is a way of honoring what we have received in our prayer and asking for more. Our sense of consolation often increases, and we may gain clarity over any sense of desolation. Return to a practice either where you had a strong emotional resonance or dissonance or where you didn't experience anything at all. In the former case, we are connecting to where the energy was sparked in us. In the latter, we are giving an opportunity for grace to enter where we did not experience it previously.

You can also bring a handful of potential words into this next section of the journey. The practices will help you continue to listen and deepen into the word calling to you. It might even end up being a phrase that combines several of your possible words.

If your word has arrived, allow it to continue to ripen in the coming days. Resist making a declaration just yet and see what continues to unfold when you give it space. Test it to see if it really rings true for you. These next ten days of practices are about sitting with the word that has come and not holding a strong attachment to it. See if the word lands in a solid place in your heart and beckons you to a journey.

To help inspire you, here are a few more examples of words that chose various members of our community:

Relentless is my word for 2023 and I just love it. I have chosen to be relentless in my pursuit of art. Today I went to gather some dishes for my refugee family and the fellow parishioner said I also have these art supplies are you interested for yourself. I ended up with paints. journals, watercolour brushes everything I needed. I am relentlessly putting out in the quantum field everything I need and it's working. Yahoo. I am about to teach art journaling to our local Wellspring group dedicated to people living with cancer and I am so ready. (Margie O'Connor)

The word that chose me is "*Fun*!" :-) I'm surprised! A bit shy to write it here! However, my eyes sparkle when I think of it, and my heart opens with joy . . . I'm taking that as a very good sign. (JoRene)

Wonderment was the word that came to me. It is present everywhere I look . . . from the colors that emerge in sunset and sunrise, the stars that are always present but are only seen in the darkness. Wonder is present when realizing that every cell in our body knows its own special duty to keep us in balance. And the wonderful way each plant and blade of grass awakens at just the right moment to grow. Wonderment is all around me to be noticed every moment! (Janith Shoning-Griffith)

11

Allow the Word to Ripen

The great poet Rainer Maria Rilke writes, "In my ripening / ripens / what you are." This may be a slow process. If you hear a word calling, sit with it for a few days. Listen attentively to the stirrings of your heart in response. Eventually there will be a tugging inside of you where you feel yourself drawn again and again to this word. You may even start to encounter synchronicities that help to confirm it for you.

Allow yourself to be in a space of unknowing with this and practice being present to your anticipation, knowing that things of the soul unfold in their own time. This is a journey of transformation, and the word may not make immediate sense to you, but trust that, over time, more of its meaning will be revealed.

I love the image of ripening as an organic and slow process. Discernment calls us to tend to those moments of ripeness, as well as those times we want to pluck the fruit before it is ready, when it hasn't developed its full sweetness.

The ancient Christian monastic traditions, especially desert, Celtic, and Benedictine, offer great wisdom for this journey of unfolding. They understood that the soul's ripening is never to be rushed and takes a lifetime of work. The gift of the contemplative path is a profound honoring of the grace of slowness.

We can grow impatient when life doesn't offer us instant insights or gratification. We call on the wisdom of these monks to accompany us, to teach us what it means to honor the beauty of waiting and attending and witnessing what it is that wants to emerge, rather than what our rational minds want to make happen. The soul always offers us more richness than we can imagine if we only make space and listen.

There hopefully comes a time in our lives when we have to admit that our own plans for our lives are not nearly as interesting as how our lives long to unfold, that these plans are "too small for me to live," as David Whyte writes in his poem "What to Remember When Awakening." Perhaps you are a recovering planner, now making more space for how the Spirit wants to move through your life and lure you forward.

The rhythms of the seasons play a significant role in my own discernment. Honoring the flowering of spring and the fruitfulness of summer, alongside the release of autumn and the stillness of winter, cultivates a way of being in the world that feels deeply reverential of my body and soul's own natural cycles. We live in a culture that glorifies spring and summer energies, but autumn and winter are just as essential for rhythms of release, rest, and incubation. When we allow the soul's slow ripening, we honor that we need to come into the fullness of our own sweetness before we pluck the fruit. This takes time and patience.

Meditation: Stages of Ripening

Allow a few moments to slow yourself down and deepen your breath. Bring your awareness from your thoughts, which is often a place of grasping and making things happen, to your heart, which is a place of receiving and attuning.

Sit in this sanctuary of the heart, allowing a few moments for being. Connect to the divine presence within.

Imagine yourself sitting by a patch of fertile soil. Spend some time inhaling the fragrance of the earth: gaze on its rich darkness, feel its moistness between your fingers. Imagine the word you have received is a seed that you are going to plant here. Create a little hole in the soil and place the seed in the cool, damp earth. Cover it over gently, sending blessings for it to grow and blossom.

Sit for a while next to your planted seed as it incubates in the womb space of darkness. Witness as it slowly begins to poke through a green tendril, reaching upward for sunlight. See it begin to emerge and take shape and form, allowing water and light to nourish it. Witness the full cycle of its growth and notice what kind of plant it becomes—perhaps a flower, fruit, vegetable, or herb—and notice your body's responses as it comes into fullness and flourishes. How does your word grow and move before you and in you? This is an act of imagination, and trust the images that come. Notice if this feels like the word you want to spend time with in the season to come.

Be present, too, as the plant begins to move toward release and decline, whether surrendering its leaves as on a tree in autumn or its whole body as the plant dries and turns to seeds for the future. Witness the fullness of this cycle and see the seeds and compost fall to the ground. See how it nourishes future growth to come.

Once your word has moved through a full cycle of emergence, growth, fullness, and decay, sit with what you have noticed in this journey. Ask yourself if this word feels like it has nourishment to offer you throughout its cycle of growth and gift.

Return to the room you are in and allow some time to journal what you have discovered. Read also from these journal reflections from past participants:

> I discovered the need to tuck my heart into that black fertile soil. That surprised me. It moved me. (My word has been *move*.) The more I held that image, the more I realized that my heart needs a little watering and tending—it feels a bit parched, I think.
>
> A line above shimmers, or hovers, for me, which I have altered, to convert it into an intention: "Cultivate a way of being in the world that feels deeply reverential of my body, heart (added) and soul's own natural cycles." (Ingrid Cyros)
>
> As much as I was "proud" of my emerging words, the truth is my dialoguing basket (longanimity, perseverance, flow) has felt a little forced. It's like I've been asking my words to DO something for me, or to MAKE something happen in me. As I navigate uncertainty at the moment, I loved the contours of this exercise . . . and considering the lifecycle of a word. It brought to mind images of seeds and darkness and gestation.
>
> The concept of ripening itself jumped out. It helped me move beyond the seed metaphor to the LIFE of that acorn and oak. Being without goals can be just as directed and meaningful an existence as

striving for outcomes—perhaps even more so. Ripening (as a guiding principle) may in fact be presenting the wisdom and longevity and wholeness I'm seeking in my life right now. I will support its dance with my other words . . . I think she will be the music. (Bridget O'Grady)

12

Trust What You Love

Jungian analyst and wise woman Clarissa Pinkola Estés writes, "It is said that all you are seeking is also seeking you. That is, if you lie still, sit still, it will find you. It has been waiting for you for a long time. Once it is here, don't move away. Rest. See what happens next."

We have such a desire to seek, strive, reach, make things happen. Our journey so far in this pilgrimage of the heart has been to learn to wait, attend, attune, and receive what comes. This is a practice of learning to trust in the love that pulses at the heart of everything. When we sit still and allow what we love to find us, when we give time for it to unfold and surprise us, we may discover deeper layers of wisdom than we knew possible. We become shaped by how we receive the word as much as by the word itself.

Preacher and mystic Howard Thurman said once in a conversation, "Don't ask yourself what the world needs. Ask yourself what makes you come alive and go do that. Because what the world needs is people who have come alive." You might be asking yourself how this word you have received contributes to the world's needs. And yet Thurman begs us to ask a different question. He prompts us to ask what makes us come alive, what sparks our heart each morning to gratitude, what gives us comfort at the end of each day, what is the one thing that feels vital to hold on to if we had to release everything else.

Twentieth-century German-language poet Rainer Maria Rilke wrote in his book *Letters to a Young Poet*, "This most of all: ask yourself in the most silent hour of your night: must I write? Dig into yourself for a deep answer. And if this answer rings out in assent, if you meet this solemn question with a strong, simple 'I must,' then build your life in accordance with this necessity; your whole life, even into its humblest and most indifferent hour, must become a sign and witness to this impulse."

Consider substituting the word *create* for the word *write* to give it a more expansive reach. What you love, what you seek, what makes you come alive, if you must pursue these things with your precious life energy, then what would it mean to build your life as "a sign and witness to this impulse"?

Almost two millennia prior to Estés writing, one of the desert elders, Abba Poemen, said, "Do not give your heart to that which does not satisfy your heart." We so often try to satisfy our hungers and longings with things that are not nourishing.

Meditation: Give Your Heart That Which Satisfies

Allow a few moments to center yourself and deepen your breath. Bring your awareness to your heart and rest in the presence of the Holy One.

Imagine that you are entering into the cave of the heart, that inner sanctuary space where we encounter the sacred within. From this place of retreat and stillness, begin to ponder the ways you try to nourish your heart. What are the things you give yourself—whether things, food, experiences, relationships, or other—that you are drawn to because you think they nourish you?

See what arises in your heart and consider each one. Does it truly nourish you? Or does it take space from that, which would be more life-giving? Be gentle and compassionate with yourself as you continue to ponder this. What are the things that fill your time and space that you could release? Imagine freeing yourself from the need to maintain these things and breathe into the space created.

Begin to let the word that has chosen you gently echo in your heart. Imagine this word has set out a feast on a table for you. What are the delicious fruits it offers to you? What sweetness does it bring to your life? When you consider your word in relationship to nourishment, does this feel like it truly brings you what you need to flourish in the season ahead?

Spend some time reflecting on these questions and noticing your body's response as well as your heart. What will enlarge you? What will bring you alive? What must you do before all else?

After a few minutes, come back to the word itself and let it echo again within you. Then allow some time to journal what you noticed or discovered.

For more inspiration, read these reflections from a past participant:

> How much time and effort have I put into things that do not nourish/satisfy my heart?
>
> I've carried Christine's question in my heart for these last few days: "What are the things that fill your time and space which you could release?" Just pondering the question has made me feel more spaciousness in my life. And when I reflect on this question with my word, "Allow the Light," echoing in my heart, I feel as though I've opened to the possibility of a new way of living. (Debra Olson-Tolar)

13

Consult the Desert Elders

The desert mothers and fathers were people who fled from the cities during early Christianity in fourth-century Egypt, Syria, and Palestine to live a more intentional life dedicated to the ongoing awareness of the divine. Their teachings were left behind in the form of short stories and sayings, much like koans in the Zen Buddhist tradition. The sayings are not always linear or logical but invitations to us to rest in paradox.

The desert monks offer us a template for how to transcend the temptations in our midst and plunge ourselves into the beating heart of life. It is up to us to translate their template into our own context.

The interior freedom that spiritual practice can bring is at the heart of the desert journey. Simplicity and humility, along with a continual mindful awareness of the presence of the divine, were some of the desert elders' core spiritual practices to help free their attachments to things and thoughts.

The desert elders each lived in a cave, hut, or single room called a cell. This was central to their journey, to retreat to solitude with the purpose of staying fully present to one's own experience. For them, the cell was an outward reality but also a metaphor for the inner life. It is a symbol for the soul work we are each called to engage in and the place of our intimate encounter with the divine.

They went to seek this kind of radical communion with the sacred presence, which teaches us that it is not the cell itself that brings inner peace. We might live in an urban center and imagine that if only we could escape to a monastery or a quiet place by the sea, then we could become present to our lives. But their wisdom reminds us that we can bring presence and focus in the midst of a crowd, and we can also sit in a silent place and be overwhelmed by thoughts and distractions.

I invite you to enter into a meditation with the wisdom of these desert ammas and abbas. You will be listening for the gifts and blessings they have to offer.

Meditation: Entering the Desert

Allow a few moments to center and breathe deeply, drawing your awareness back to yourself. Rest in the presence of the Beloved who dwells in the cave of your heart, that interior cell where you are called to simply be.

Invite in the presence of some of the desert mothers and fathers to be with you. Notice how they appear to you. Notice if one or two of them approach you, and invite them to sit with you for a while.

Share with them where you are in this season of your life and what the questions of your heart are right now. Listen for their response.

Share the journey you have been on so far to listen for your word and receive it. Tell them the word that has chosen you and ask for their wisdom.

Engage in a conversation about how to know you have received a word that will bear fruit. Open your heart to new insights.

Ask them for support and guidance on how to be more present to yourself and to your life. Share what most distracts you, whether replaying conversations in the past, planning for the future, worrying, or other things that keep your attention from being fully present.

Imagine these ammas and abbas blessing you with strength and focus. Notice how this feels in your body. They extend their hands out to you and gift you with your word written in beautiful calligraphy on a stone. Notice how it feels to receive this gift.

Offer gratitude for their presence, wisdom, and blessing, and remember you can return to be with them at any time.

Return your awareness gently back to the room you are in and allow some time to reflect on your experience.

Here is one reflection from a past participant, Eileen M. Palmer: "I'd been sitting with several words, such as *peace*, *rest*, *release*. I found this a powerful and unexpected meditation. I acutely felt the presence of the desert elders, and a couple of spiritual teachers I have travelled on pilgrimage in the desert with. I was unexpectedly given a related word, *shalom*. I can remember thinking I would google the meanings of the word, but then I was shown meanings . . . for each letter, for the shape of the word, meanings I had never before considered that were both mystical and profound."

14

Create a Pantoum

It can be very fruitful and rich to read back over your journals from this past year. This is part of my annual reflection time in the days leading up to the New Year. We can often see patterns at play from this broader perspective that we didn't notice in our day-to-day reflections.

If you aren't someone who journals regularly, you can still do this exercise with any writing you have done for this process so far. If you don't have any, then you could also engage in this process by first doing some freewriting for ten minutes in response to your word or even pulling a book off a shelf, such as a collection of poems or essays—preferably one that you really love and suspect might contain some word-related wisdom.

The French pantoum is a poetic form with a circular structure that comes from the ordered repetition of lines and creates its own rhythm and poetry in the process.

You may be someone who already loves to write poetry as part of your spiritual practice. Words and images may come easily to you. Or you may be someone for whom poetry strikes a bit of fear. The beauty of this process is that you have already written the poem. You simply need to gather the phrases and enter them in the arranged order.

Creative Practice: Write a Pantoum

To write a pantoum, spend some time reading over your old journals, or the writing you have just done, or a few pages of a favorite book. With a colored pen, circle or underline six short phrases (a few words) that shimmer for you or surprise you in some way.

Use the template below to create your French pantoum. For lines 1, 2, 3, 4, 6, and 8, you would write in one of each of the six sentences or phrases from your journals, freewriting, or reading, then follow the instructions for repeating the other lines of the poem.

Let the lines fall where they want to; try not to force this process or make something happen. The magic of it is in its serendipity.

FRENCH PANTOUM

STANZA 1:

Line 1 (new line): ____________________
Line 2 (new line): _____________________
Line 3 (new line): _____________________
Line 4 (new line): _____________________

STANZA 2:

Line 5 (repeat of line 2 in stanza 1): _____________________
Line 6 (new line): _____________________
Line 7 (repeat of line 4 in stanza 1): _____________________
Line 8 (new line): _____________________

STANZA 3:

Line 9 (repeat line 6 of stanza 2): _______________
Line 10 (repeat line 3 of the first stanza): _________________
Line 11 (repeat line 8 of stanza 2): ______________
Line 12 (repeat line 1 of the first stanza): ___________________

Then give your pantoum a title of the word that has chosen you. When you feel complete, read the poem aloud.

Providing a structure is a helpful way to introduce writing poetry to someone unfamiliar with it. The repeating form of the pantoum can have a deepening effect. Notice what it is like to hear your words and images repeated again and again. How does it draw you deeper into the experience? How might this poem shed light on the word that has chosen you? Does it deepen its meaning or help it to ripen?

Be inspired by these examples from past participants:

CREATIVITY

Grant me a rich life
Which is natural which is infinite which is yes
Creativity is the natural order of life
My creativity has wintered long enough

Which is natural which is infinite which is yes
The world offers itself to your imagination
My creativity has wintered long enough
Love Your Creation through me

The world offers itself to your imagination
Creativity is the natural order of life
Love Your Creation through me
Grant me a rich life. (Meredith J. Webb)

HOSPITALITY

Full-bodied hospitality
sparkles on the web
A path of forward and through
Radiating love

Sparkles on the web
Live in the Now
Radiating love
You are not alone.

Live in the Now
A path of forward and through
You are not alone
Full-bodied hospitality. (Jeanie Robinson)

15

Take a Pilgrimage of Memory

We live in a time when most of us have smartphones and take photos daily of the moments of our lives. I know I have hundreds of images of my sweet dog Sourney, as well as many from the daily walk we take along the canal and river in the city where I live. There may be special occasions and travels recorded there too. I smile when my tablet displays random memories on my screen and delight in the serendipity and act of remembering.

For this exploration, I invite you to take some time to scroll through the images on your phone, or a regular camera (if that is how you usually take photos), or a digital photo album. Select three images that especially shimmer for you or challenge you in some way. This is an act of discernment to choose.

Once you have your images selected, I invite you to move through the practice of *visio divina*, or sacred seeing, with each one. The guidelines are below, and you can modify them as needed for time. Enter fully into the landscape of each image, its textures, its colors, what it evokes in your heart.

Meditation: *Visio Divina*

Settling and Shimmering

Close your eyes and prepare yourself for prayer by connecting to your body and breath, gently deepening the rhythm of your breath, bringing your awareness to your heart center. As you breathe in, imagine receiving the gift of vision, the sacred ability to see deeply below the surface of things. As you breathe out, imagine being able to allow your eyes to communicate love to others and to what you gaze on. Allow a few moments to rest into this nourishing rhythm of preparing your eyes to behold what is before you.

Gently open your eyes and softly gaze on the image with "eyes of the heart." This is a gentle receiving gaze, not a hard, penetrating stare. Move your eyes over the image, taking in all of the colors, shapes, and symbols. Bring a sense of curiosity to this image, exploring it with reverence, noticing all of its textures and features that come with seeing it more closely.

As your eyes wander around the image in a brief visual pilgrimage, notice if there is someplace on the image that shimmers for you, somewhere that is stirring energy for you. Allow your eyes to rest gently there.

Savoring and Stirring

Be present to this place on the image that is calling for more attention. Begin to open your imagination to memories and other images that want to stir in you in response. Allow this place, these symbols or colors, to unfold and open you to other connections. Notice if there are any feelings stirring within you and connect to your breath again, making room for whatever wants to move through you in this time.

Summoning and Serving

As the image moves your heart, begin to listen for how you are being invited in this moment of your life out of this time of prayer. Make space for your heart to be touched and for a longing to respond to the sacred call to move in you. Notice if the invitation wants to emerge perhaps as an image or a symbol instead of in words. Ask how your life is becoming a work of art and how you are called to claim your place as the artist of this masterpiece. Where in your life are you called to bring more color, to bring more mystery, to explore what the artwork of your life wants you to discover?

Slowing and Stilling

Close your eyes if they are still open and release the images you have been gazing on. Sink into stillness, slow your breath down, and rest in the grace of being for several minutes.

When you are ready to end your time of prayer, connect with your breath again and gently bring your awareness back to the room, maintaining eyes of the heart. Following your prayer, sometimes it can be helpful to gaze one more time on the image, taking it all in again and seeing if you notice anything new. Then offer a moment of gratitude for the way this image has touched your heart.

To close this prayer, allow a few minutes to journal what you noticed or discovered. What does this image have to say about the season of life you are in? How does this image reflect or not reflect some aspect of the word that has chosen you?

You can let this be the whole practice or, if you feel inspired, move through the process again with one or two more images.

Past participants described their experience of this meditation in this way:

> I picked 4 photos saved in my photo library—all were memes or others' inspired photos. I found as I prayed with them that my heart opened as I prayed

confirming my choice of words for next year. First a grandmother playing with her grandchild, second a little girl dancing, third an angelic figure on water amidst the moon and stars and lastly prayer candle stands all in a row full of lit candles, melted wax—prayers lifted to God. Delight and frolic as I play with my grandchildren; dancing joy; my connection with angels and contemplative and intercessory prayer. Each of these are who I am now and who I am called to be! All life-giving! An amazing experience! (Lynne Jensen)

I'm a cat person. I adopted Bodhi and Grazie from a shelter, not siblings but bonding first with each other to feel safe. We're a family now. I chose pictures of them because they fill my heart with love, also whimsy. They make me laugh, and I love laughter. My favorite is the first picture where they are stretching and reaching out (but not for a word, we're all letting it come to us). It feels like a movement, a dance, to be home. I now know my word, *cadence*, and it has been a movement, a dance, for me to be home in this time in my life. (Patia Carque)

16

Attune to Your Body's Wisdom

Many of us have been exiles from our bodies—our holy bodies, our beautiful bodies, our bodies created lovingly by God and sustained and nourished by the earth.

In our rush through life, we neglect the body's wisdom. We work through fatigue and illness, pushing our bodies and feeling frustrated when they don't keep up. Or we look at our physical selves with disdain when parts don't measure up to some external standard (which is always designed to sell us something).

God became flesh. The Christian teaching of the Incarnation points to embodiment as one of the most important spiritual journeys we make, and it is impacted on multiple levels. It determines our relationship to time—do we rush through our lives or savor slowness? It helps us to resist consumerism and the constant quest for self-improvement and rest in the beauty and bounty of our bodies.

It impacts our relationships with food—do we eat just to fill our hunger, to fill an emptiness, or to truly nourish ourselves? Also the earth—do we see ourselves as separate from the earth or in intimate communion? And even our journeys of healing—do we seek the quick fix or cure and lose patience with the slow process of healing?

The Christian monastic tradition has left an unfortunate legacy of body denial. And yet the very contemplative practices that are so nourishing for our souls can also be directed toward our bodies as a way of plunging into and celebrating the depths of our embodied beings. If we believe that God became flesh, how might we take the Incarnation seriously by entering into intimacy with our own bodies?

In his book *Touching Enlightenment*, Buddhist author Reginald Ray says the body is the last unexplored wilderness. He believes that many meditation practices keep us firmly anchored in our heads. The ancient desert mothers and fathers journeyed out to the wildness of the desert to find God there, at the edges of life, in the places where they felt uncomfortable, and God was allowed to be as expansive as possible. In my longing to grow more intimate with the gift of my body, I feel a deeper kinship with those ancient monks called out to the wild edges to discover new ways of being with God. As Ray suggests, our bodies are a wondrous wilderness just waiting for our attention.

The wilderness calls us to be with life's messiness, to relinquish our desire to control what is happening and enter wholeheartedly into life's unfolding. Movement becomes a sacred medicine that heals the disconnection so many of us experience day after day from our beautiful bodies. It is a medicine that helps us to address the places we feel blocked or afraid and allows us to honor those experiences and dance beyond their confinement. As we dance, we discover places of rigidity and holding, stiffness and pain. We can respond with gentleness and opening.

Meditation: Dancing with Your Word

I invite you to make some time to dance with your word for the year. Choose a piece of music that feels supportive to where you are right now. It could be a slow instrumental piece or something with lyrics that perhaps reflects the wisdom of your word for you.

If dance feels like too much, think of it as a gentle movement meditation. You are in full control of how quiet or expressive your dance is, how long or how short.

When you dance, I recommend creating a sacred space. This might mean an altar. Even just lighting a candle can signal your intention to make this practice a prayer rather than merely an "exercise." When your intention is to enter into the wisdom of your body, and to allow your body, as much as possible, unimpeded movement as an expression of unnamed desires, it is a prayer and a holy act.

If you are in too much pain to dance, try dancing in your imagination. Find a quiet place to lie down, put on a piece of music, and then imagine yourself dancing. There is a physical effect. Or you can try just dancing with one hand.

When you feel stuck as to how to move, try just shaking your body. Animals shake to reorganize and calm their nervous systems and to shake off stressful experiences. Begin by shaking one hand as vigorously as you can, then the other. Then shake one leg while bracing against a wall. Then shake the other leg. Then shake out what you sit on. Shake out your voice by vocalizing some sounds. You might imagine as you are shaking that you are setting free whatever you don't need to hold on to.

You can return to stillness at any time needed. Always honor your body's limits.

Move the word into your body. Let yourself dance to the word that is rising up and see how your body responds. Play a piece of music and see if words emerge in the dancing. Let your body lead this prayer. Release the thinking, planning, organizing mind.

After your dance feels complete, allow a few minutes first to simply be in silence and notice how the energy is moving through your body. Then take a pen and write down any reflections that have been stirred or use some colored pens to draw expressively on a blank piece of paper. What new dimensions of your word emerged?

17

Listen to the Elements

When we recognize ourselves as a part of the earth community, as the Scriptures and mystics have encouraged us to do for centuries, then we begin to see the profound mystery at work in the depths of our own souls as the same sacred mystery at work in the natural world. Being present to the gifts of creation helps to give us insights into paths for our own spiritual growth and into the nature of how God is present to us.

Each of the elements offers us a unique energy or way of understanding the sacred: water flows and cleanses, the earth roots us and nourishes us, fire represents the burning of love and passion, and wind expresses freedom, breath, and unpredictability.

The elements also are held in tension with each other in terms of the quality they represent. We typically consider fire and water as opposites and earth and air as opposites. This tension invites us to also pray with the elements toward a reconciliation of the paradoxes of the world and uniting the opposing forces within us in our soul's quest for integration and wholeness.

By bringing the four elements into our prayer, we can cultivate two primary connections: First, by rooting our prayer in connection with the elements, we begin to forge an awareness of how much we are a part of creation and share in earth's elements as well. We may begin to experience ourselves as a part of the matrix of the natural world and as creatures just like other creatures.

Second, in opening ourselves to the metaphors that the elements offer us for how God works in the world, we discover a God who dwells at the heart of all living things, who sustains and transforms creation moment by moment, and who is an indispensable presence in the world. Reflecting on the nature of God in connection with the four elements helps to anchor our sense of the sacred presence right in our midst of the everyday and reveals a God whose immanence shimmers through creation.

Praying with the elements encourages your spiritual path and practice to be fully embodied through this wondrous world with which we have been gifted. This means practicing gratitude for the abundant gifts of God symbolized in the elements and rooting prayer in a sense of all of creation as a great sacrament or window onto the holy. By allowing the qualities of the elements to become part of our prayer, we can recognize God's active work in creation since the very beginning of time.

I invite you into a meditation where you will pray with the energy and quality of each of the four elements, listening for what wisdom they might offer for living with your word into the year ahead. I connect each element to a particular direction and time of day, which reflects the wisdom of Celtic tradition as well as some Indigenous American traditions such as Cherokee.

Meditation: Letting the Elements Speak Wisdom to Your Word

Begin by centering yourself through the breath. Draw your breath deeply and slowly in and out. Imagine your awareness coming to rest in your heart center. This is a time of prayer and not figuring things out. Open your heart to receive what gifts may come.

Plant your word like a seed in your heart, letting it be a guiding intention for this time of reflection and meditation.

Begin with the element of air and breath, connected to the direction of the East and the rising sun in Celtic tradition. It evokes the energy of spring blossoming and the waxing moon, burgeoning toward its own fullness. Let this quality of dawn and new beginnings infuse you as you breathe in deeply for three slow breaths.

Imagine your own breath linking you to the breath of all living creatures. See the dance of breath with each exhale: the plants take in the carbon dioxide and release oxygen; inhale and receive that gift offered.

In what ways might your word for the year be a gateway to a new awakening? How could it help you breathe more fully into your days?

We move to the element of fire, connected to the direction of the South and the midday sun. Fire invites us to tend our own journey of claiming the height of our passions and what desires burn brightly in our hearts. This element is also connected to the energy of summer's ripeness and the full moon.

Reconnect with your heart, the place of passion ignited and what the mystics call "the living flame of love." Bring compassion to yourself, to your loved ones, to your community, to the world.

How might this word for the year help to kindle and sustain your inner fire? What are you being invited to say yes to? In what ways do you long to burn more brightly?

Turn your attention to the element of water, which is connected to the direction of the West and the setting sun. It invites us to release ourselves into life's flow rather than forcing our own will on life. This element is also connected to autumn's surrender and the waning moon. Imagine facing the direction of the West, the hour of waning light and endings, the time when we realize that time is limited. Water invites us to yield to the flow of our lives, to let our lives be organic.

What is your word for the year calling you to release and surrender? How is it inviting you to step into the flow of life?

Finally, we turn to the element of earth. Earth is connected to the direction of the North and the hour of midnight. It invites us to move into unknowing, darkness, and rest. This element is connected to winter's time of hibernation and the new moon.

The earth element invites us into mystery and letting go of our need to understand everything, the invitation to rest fully.

Return your awareness to your own sacred center and rest in the presence of these wisdom guides. Offer gratitude for the gifts of wind, fire, water, and earth as spiritual directors for your journey. Spend a few minutes with your journal, making note of the elements that called to you the most and which ones you felt the most resistance to.

Here's what stood out to past participants:

I resonate with the element of water in today's practice. I feel like it accompanies my current journey of continuous surrendering, a beautiful and sometimes unsettling dance between my willfulness (my trying to make things happen) and willingness (my allowing things to happen). What arises is an invitation to embody the way of the water—trusting in its own potential while allowing the path to shape it. (Jo-ed Tome)

From spring and the east, the wind and the beginning of things back to winter when all is darkness and rest and incubation and dormancy and mystery and deep in the earth . . . those resonated most to me in this moment concerning the word DELIGHT. . . . I don't know what it will be, what it will become and I don't want to know either . . . waiting upon the holy surprises that will come forth. (Betsy Retallack)

18

Embark on a Photography Pilgrimage

I introduced you to contemplative walks in the first section. These are walks where your sole focus is on being present to each moment's invitation as it unfolds rather than setting out with a particular goal. There is nowhere to "get to." You begin by breathing deeply and centering yourself, bringing your awareness down to your heart center. The first walk I invited you on was a time of listening for the word; now that you have received your word, you can go on a walk and let your word continue to ripen and unfold. Let the world around you speak to you of your word's meaning and wisdom.

The contemplative dimension of this is reflected in the space we allow without agenda or rushing. When we let the experience unfold rather than making something happen, we are attuning to a particular way of being. In this slowness, we hear a deeper voice speaking. We shift from the stance of taking to receiving. We bring this to our camera as well, and we wait for images to arrive as gifts rather than seeking to capture every moment through the lens. In my book *Eyes of the Heart: Photography as a Contemplative Practice*, I write about the difference between "taking" photos and "receiving" them. The first is reflective of our consumerist, grasping, scarcity-focused mindset, so prevalent in Western culture. The second is the call of the monk and mystic, the contemplative, the one in us who sees all of life as gift and so receives the graces offered with a sense of wonder and gratitude. It is the difference between walking around with closed fists and open palms.

If you have yet to receive your word, you can still go on the contemplative walk and allow moments to call to you. Let the frame of your camera help you to discern what to include and what to leave out of the frame. In this practice, perhaps the hint of a word emerges.

If you are physically unable to walk, you could sit on a bench outside or gaze out of a window and behold the beauty around you.

Meditation: Contemplative Walk

Begin by allowing a few moments to center yourself and deepen your breathing. Bring yourself present to the moment and plant your word for the year in your heart, letting it take root there. You will hold it gently as you walk through the world.

Go out in the world for a walk; it could be just down your block or in a nearby park. Bring a camera; a simple camera on your phone is fine. As you walk, stay present to the world as a sacred text, much like you would in *lectio divina* with the Scriptures.

Repeat your word to yourself as you walk. If you created a breath prayer, consider praying that as you go. Pay attention to moments that call to you, especially those that feel like they have a resonance with your word. You don't need to explain why or how; trust your intuition.

With your camera, receive images that deepen your experience. Open your hands wide and pay attention to what gifts and graces arrive when we move through the world in an openhearted way. The frame of the lens helps you to see them in new ways and reflect again later on what you have encountered.

Your invitation is to walk and be open to noticing all moments when your word seems to shimmer in some way in the world around you. Let this be a journey of discovery. See what you notice as you bring this awareness with you. As you encounter each moment, use your camera to receive an image of it to carry with you. Notice which moments stir your heart especially.

Is there a bird, a tree, a leaf, a flower, a door or window, or a sign that sparks your heart?

When you return home, see if one of these images speaks especially to your heart and rest with it for a while. What might it reveal about an invitation in this season of your life?

19

Call on the Angels, Saints, and Ancestors

In many of our spiritual traditions, there is a belief that spiritual beings dwell on the other side of the veil between worlds. These angels, saints, and ancestors are available to us, reaching out to us to connect and support and guide us. These beings are a force of great love in the world and help us to remember we are never alone.

Love is the primal force behind what we do and how we live. We create art to understand more deeply what it means to be human. Part of what makes life worth living is our passion, our desire to be in relationship—with ourselves, with our beloveds, with the divine. When we open our hearts to the blessings of the angels, saints, and our ancestors, we open a river of love.

When we abide in love, we can experience a sense of union with all there is. It is the source of spirituality, especially the mystical paths found in all religious traditions, a sense of the ultimate oneness of everything that is, and seeking to experience that unity in daily life. Love calls us into connection with the world. In times when feeling disconnection and isolation is easier than ever, love calls us to step into the flesh-and-blood relationships, to engage, to risk, to be vulnerable.

Spiritual writer Joyce Rupp, in her book *Fragments of Your Ancient Name*, writes that a lineage of ancestors walks in front of us: "They mark the path with their wisdom, / Fill the air with fragrant goodness."

One of the great gifts of making these conscious connections and opening to these presences available to all of us is a deepened sense of community over time. The angels, saints, and ancestors are all cheering us on, sending us love and more love, and asking us to spread it far and wide, to not hold back.

Angels are beings of light. They surround us with love's protection. Saints are the holy ones who have embraced love as their path and witness to how we, too, can follow them. Ancestors are both those wise and well ones who have stepped fully into love and also those still wounded ones aching for the healing that love brings. They remind us of our own humanity. They reveal stories of who we truly are, the longings that beat in our blood.

Sometimes when life feels lonely or challenging in other ways, it can be hard to remember the love of thousands that shimmers just behind the veil between worlds.

The angels, saints, and ancestors—and the love of those thousands—are already awaiting us. We need to simply turn our attention and gaze toward them. We can ask them for their blessings on us, on our lives, on the word that has come to guide us for the year ahead.

Meditation: Experiencing the Love of Thousands

Slow down your breath and gently arrive fully to your body. Notice if your body needs anything for more ease right now. Let your breath guide your awareness from your head to your heart. Enter into this inner sanctuary space and feel yourself in the presence of the Holy One, whose flame dwells with you always. Offer a moment of gratitude for this deep knowing and connection to the source of all that is. Call your word to mind and let it take root in your heart again as a guide.

Call in the presence first of the archangels Michael, Gabriel, Uriel, and Raphael to bring their light of protection, communication, wisdom, and healing to your life right now. Ask your guardian angel to surround you with care. Ask for their wisdom around the word you have received. What new layers of insight do they have to offer?

Invite in the presence of the communion of saints—human, animal, and mineral—to be with you as well and feel the radiance of their love. Notice the energy of the space you inhabit. Call forth any patron or especially loved saints. Ask them to shower you with their wisdom for this next season of your life and make space for what they want to offer you. Listen for what they have to say about your word.

Invite in all of the wise and well ancestors to surround you, those both known to you and the thousands of unknown ancestors who loved, laughed, struggled, grieved, raged, danced, and endured so you could be here. Feel their strength and resilience surrounding you and flowing through your blood and bone. Know this gift in your body as much as possible. Ask them what they want you to know as you continue onward.

See them all raising their hands in blessing and showering golden light all around you.

Deepen your breath and slowly return to your physical body and the room you are in. Spend some time with a journal writing down anything you want to remember.

A past participant remembered this:

I loved the feeling of being surrounded by the archangels. That felt good. I asked Julian of Norwich what she could add to my word—rest—and I found this: He is our only true rest. And he wishes to be known. He wants us to rest in him. He is all that is, and he knows that anything less is not enough for us. This is why no soul can find peace until it empties itself of all forms. Only when the soul has willingly become nothing, out for love of him who is everything, can it find true rest. Rest is peace through surrender. I love this extra layer as it isn't just stopping but putting off of things (not sure what yet) to find peace or true rest. (Sarah Pickering)

20

Bring Your Word to a Threshold Place

Thresholds are the space between, when we move from one time to another, as in the threshold of dawn to day or of dusk to dark; one space to another as in times of inner or outer journeying or pilgrimage; one awareness to another as in times when our old structures start to fall away, and we begin to build something new. The Celts describe thresholds as "thin times or places" where heaven and earth are closer together and the veil between worlds is thin.

In the Celtic imagination, thresholds are potent places. We experience the thresholds of the year unfolding so that each new season beckons us into a renewed awareness of the nearness of the holy presence. In the Celtic wheel of the year, there are eight portals in time that mark the equinoxes and solstices, as well as the midway points between them. Each of these festivals hold the possibility of deeper connection to the divine. Beginning a new year is another kind of threshold.

We encounter thresholds each day through the movement across the hinges of time. Early morning and evening's turnings were thought to be especially graced times of day when the otherworld was near.

There are physical places that evoke a sense of wonder—sacred sites where thousands of pilgrims have visited and prayed because of the numinous quality of these places.

We encounter thresholds in our experience as well. Those times when life shifts, sometimes out of choice and often because of circumstance. Sometimes this is because of illness or loss; sometimes we move to a new home or start a new job. Sometimes we simply feel that we are on the edge of the old and the new. We are forever crossing thresholds in our lives, both the literal kind when moving through doorways, leaving the building, or going to another room and the metaphorical thresholds, when time becomes a transition space of waiting and tending. We hope for news about a friend struggling with illness; we long for clarity about our own deepest dreams.

If you are in a place of discernment in your life, a season of pondering next steps, then you are on a threshold as well. Thresholds are liminal times when the past season has come to a close, but there is a profound unknowing of what will come next.

Thresholds are challenging because they demand that we step into the in-between place of letting go of what has been while awaiting what is still to come. When we are able to fully release our need to control the outcome, thresholds become rich and graced places of transformation. We can only become something new when we have released the old faces we have been wearing, even if it means not knowing quite who we are in the space between.

Meditation: Thresholds and Discernment

Think about the various physical and symbolic thresholds in your life and all the times you cross a threshold. This might be from one space to another, across a doorway, from one activity to another, or tending the thresholds of the day, especially at dawn and dusk.

Wander out to an edge place; it could be as simple as the boundary of your property or even your own front door. Or perhaps you live near a river bank, a shoreline, or where the forest begins. Carry your word for the year with you. Breathe it in and out with every step.

Thresholds are as much imaginal places as they are literal and physical ones. As spiritual seekers, we are called to live with one foot in the world of earthy and everyday experience. The other foot is in the transcendent realm, where the divine breaks through our ordinary consciousness. To hold this kind of imaginal awareness is to recognize heaven on earth and Paradise breaking through in each moment.

When we are in discernment, it means keeping an eye attuned to the ways that the holy touches us through experience. We can cultivate the capacity to see another layer of reality at work. We can listen for symbols and encounters with this numinosity because it happens within the very deepest recesses of our souls. To allow the soul's slow ripening asks that we sit in the mystery at times, awaiting the moment of fullness.

Stand at a threshold with your word. Imagine the ways the word helps you to release the old, what is no longer needed or serving you. Bless the releasing and send those things on their way.

Then imagine the ways the word helps you to welcome in the new, to await the dreaming of your life into the days ahead. How does your word help you dwell in this space of possibility with hopefulness?

When you have completed the experience, return home and allow some time to reflect on what you encountered and heard.

Past participants described their encounters in this way:

> I'm overjoyed thinking of the ways my word for the year ("Allow the Light") will help guide me in releasing that which no longer serves me and in embracing the new. Standing on the threshold of this new year I am hopeful and am able to sit in the mystery. This has not been my pattern in the past. I like knowing what's coming, I like making plans. I have a deep feeling that my word will teach me the value of not knowing! (Debra Olson-Tolar)

> My word "connectedness" gives me the courage to wait patiently in this liminal space where I am at the moment, a newly retiree from the corporate world, at 70 wondering what lies ahead. My word brings me in a posture of gratitude for all the infinite possibilities beyond the doors of the past and a posture of expectancy ("preemptive joy"?) of what lies ahead. Frees me from the constant dialogue of "what could have been" and "forethought of grief" (Wendell Berry's word). Connectedness is ever present in the NOW!
>
> Changes the landscape of Life, not only providing a new lens to view things, but is a gift of new eyes to see, behold and gaze! (Jose "Joe" Albaniel)

Interlude

Hermit

In the winter of 2017, I came down with the flu just before the holidays, which amplified the mood of going inward between Christmas and Epiphany, a time of reflection for me. We had had a very full fall leading pilgrimage groups and then moving house in Galway, where we live in Ireland.

We had a foster dog over the holidays, a little Jack Russell / chihuahua mix we have named Sisi. In Ireland, the pounds all close for two weeks over Christmas and New Year's, so the rescue groups put out a plea for folks to foster during this time to make more room for incoming dogs so they don't have to be put to sleep. This is our quiet time of year, so two years prior, we fostered little Ginger Nut (who was then reunited with her owners), the previous year was Melba (who found a wonderful new home), and that year was Sisi. Those of you who have animal companions in your life know the gift and grace they offer, the witness to another way of being. They are definitely the original monks. My favorite moments were her sweet, snuggly presence while I journal or nap.

In the midst of all of this, I had been listening for my word for 2017. My word almost always arrives slowly for me. I had thought it might be *nest* as being in our own home felt like an important threshold in our journey here in Ireland. A deep rooting down. But it wasn't landing fully, so I waited. I tried on several other words, including my word from the previous year, *surplus*, which, at the time, I didn't think was quite done with me but still didn't feel like *my* word for the year to come.

Finally, it came one afternoon during a long nap, in that place between waking and sleeping, I realized I was savoring my hermit time. When I heard *hermit* in my mind, I remembered being at Holy Hill Hermitage in Sligo the previous fall and how I loved their rhythm of life, which allowed for hermit days and also days when they could tend to the demands of life and earning a living. I was inspired by the balance they committed themselves to and thought that was something I could do. So, in this dream space, *hermit* shimmered. I also felt some resistance to the challenges it offers, which made me believe even more strongly it had a lot to teach me in the year to come.

While I feel incredibly privileged to lead the life I do and to live in Ireland, and at the time I was traveling a lot for work and lead groups, I was being drawn more and more to a stability of place again—to really commit to the landscape, the stories, the people, the plants. I was being drawn more deeply home. And like the hermit, to seek time of solitude and silence to simply listen.

I already was keeping Sabbath each week with John, but the word was calling me to a full hermit day each week for time alone as well, as much as possible, and schedule in some longer silent retreats before my time filled up. To make this my first priority again. Time to really enter into the gifts of silence and solitude.

I love this quote from Meister Eckhart: "I need to be silent for a while, worlds are forming in my heart." I have often leaned into these words before when I feel the longing for a retreat rise up. I trust all of this, trusting that it led me in a holy direction.

Part Three

Carry the Word with You

Now that you have received a word and let it ripen, prayed with it, and listened to its wisdom for you, we will focus in this last section on ways to carry the word with you into the year ahead. You will be invited to create poems and images and songs to help inspire you. Make a regular practice of praying with your word, letting it dwell in your heart, and seeing how it speaks to the events of your day. These practices are meant to help you integrate the word as a foundation of your spiritual life for the weeks and months to come.

Imagine your word is like a treasure to carry with you each day. Enfold it with care and unwrap it in quiet moments or moments of transition between activities, letting it speak to you. Behold it shimmering before you, full of promise and wisdom.

21

Create a Breath Prayer

Many religious traditions have some version of breath prayer. In the Christian tradition, the roots of breath prayer are built from Saint Paul's invitation to people who hold faith to "pray without ceasing." In early Christianity, many monks and nuns would endeavor to do exactly this in practice by bringing prayer to each breath. They would combine a phrase of prayer or blessing with the inhale and exhale so that every breath was a chance for them to be present to the sacred.

This kind of mantra practice has also long been present in the Hindu tradition, where a sacred phrase is repeated as an anchor to keep one's awareness focused on the divine at work in the world. In the Buddhist tradition, these take the form of gathas, short verses recited with the breath as part of mindfulness practice and meditation and recited during ordinary activities like walking, working, or cleaning and so on.

In the *Philokalia*, the great collection of Eastern Christian wisdom books, which also teaches about the early practice of the Jesus prayer, Saint Hesychios the priest writes, "Let the name of Jesus adhere to your breath, and then you will know the blessings of stillness." I love this image of letting the prayer adhere to your breath. Rather than a forcing together of word and breath, imagine the words naturally being drawn to the breath like a magnet to metal or like bees to flowers. In this bringing together, the "blessings of stillness" wash over you.

Our breath is such an intimate companion, one that sustains us moment by moment, even as we are entirely unaware of that sustaining gift. Yet when we bring our intention to it, it also becomes an ally for slowing down, for touching stillness.

Meditation: Compose Your Own Breath Prayer

I invite you to create a breath prayer that incorporates your word for the year into it or evokes the word for you.

There are two main ways you might approach this: The first is to call the activity to mind and heart, listening for what the prayer is you want to offer while engaging in it. This might be a simple prayer for becoming more present to the moment, or it might be a prayer for how this activity has the potential to transform you and your awareness. Both are wonderful ways to approach things. The activity has value in itself, and each moment is a doorway to transformation, to seeing life in a new way. You can experiment with the words and then link them to your inhale and exhale. Then practice your new breath prayer whenever you can, resting on the words you created to support you. You might also engage in this activity and ask the divine to inspire you with the right words, asking for help and support in creating the prayer that will be nourishing.

The other way to do this is to keep alert to lines from Scripture or poems that inspire you. Sometimes a phrase arrives to us in a way that feels like a gift. You can then draw on this phrase to create a breath prayer and consider which activity it might be in support of.

Then create a simple phrase that can be divided in two—the first half on the in-breath and the second half on the out-breath.

Years ago, for example, I fell in love with David Whyte's poem "What to Remember When Waking," and the line "what you can plan is too small for you to live" felt luminous for me as a recovering planner. Soon it became a mantra for me. I found myself often breathing it in, *what I can plan*, then breathing out *is too small for me*, adapting the words slightly for my prayer. I often prayed this prayer when I found myself trying to figure things out too much, trying to control how things unfolded.

Perhaps there is a poem or reading that already includes your word that could be the source for a breath prayer. But also open to your own words, the prayers of your heart that rise up and want to honor particular activities that feel integral to your day. Let those words bless and reveal the way the sacred is already present to you.

Then make a commitment to practice this breath prayer for a few minutes at the start of each day, as a way to root yourself in the word and its wisdom.

For inspiration, reflect on these breath prayers from past participants:

> My word is *flow*. A favorite hymn and one sung at a close friend's memorial service is "How Can I Keep From Singing?" These words and the melody are especially meaningful: My life flows on in endless song above earth's lamentation. My breath prayer: *Inhale—my life flows on, Exhale—in endless song.* (Carol Cherry)

> My word is *SURRENDER* . . .
> My Breath Prayer . . .

Inhale: Now is the time
Exhale: to Surrender . . .
I sense that this little breath prayer will be such a gift as I embark upon this journey into the new year with my new word. (Kristine Schnarr)

22

Choose a Spiritual Teacher

We live in a world with an abundance of choices and possibilities. Sometimes diving deep with one thing or idea is just what our heart needs to deepen and root into something more solid.

Seek out a spiritual teacher or author you can explore this coming year who might support you in deepening into this word. Maybe there is already someone who comes to mind. Perhaps you can ask a spiritual director or soul friend for their recommendations.

Perhaps it is reading all the works of mystics like Hildegard of Bingen, Howard Thurman, Thomas Merton, the desert elders or poets like Rainer Maria Rilke, Mary Oliver, or Maya Angelou.

I am currently working on a book about seven medieval women mystics and am really relishing making time to focus on each woman's writing one by one, allowing their words to nourish me and inspire new directions—to feel an intimate connection building, like a friendship across time. I offer each one the word that has chosen me for the year and then listen for their unique vision.

Maybe there is an author whose work has been calling to you. Choose one and commit to steeping in their wisdom. Then read everything you can that was written by them and let them be a companion through the year ahead, a midwife to your own holy birth and growing awareness of how this word is calling you forward across the threshold.

You might also look for a holy icon of this spiritual teacher if one is available. You can even create your own by printing out an image of them, pasting it to a piece of heavy paper, and then embellishing it in any way that feels expressive of their gifts. Keep this icon either on your altar or as a bookmark in your journal or in the current book you are reading by them.

In a world full of so many books and choices, committing to one writer might feel challenging. Maybe it even feels impossible. It doesn't mean you can't read anything or anyone else for the year, but it is a wonderful opportunity to notice if this kind of focus might bear fruit in new ways.

Meditation: Sacred Reading

Let your times of sacred reading with your spiritual teacher be a ritual and prayer. When you sit down to read, allow some time before you begin, to breathe deeply and bring your heart fully present to the moment. Then ask for the spirit of your chosen teacher to be with you in this time of reflection. Each time you sit down to be with their writings, ask what wisdom they have to offer you to deepen into your word.

You might want to keep a separate journal or notebook to track what you glean from their writings or mark the pages you write in some way to find them easily again.

Your reading can be a modified practice of *lectio divina* called *lectio continua*. The ancient monks used to commit to one book of Scripture at a time and would read through until they reached a word or phrase that shimmered for them or called out to them. Hold your word in your heart and read in a mindful way, attuned to gifts of wisdom that arrive. When you find a phrase that shimmers, write it down in your notebook and pause. Journal about any associations this brings—other words, images, feelings, or memories. Then listen for the invitation.

You can continue in your reading, repeating this process as many times as feels fruitful. The goal is not to read as much as possible in the time you have committed but to read in a fully present and reverent way.

At the end of your reading, give thanks for your teacher's guidance in this time and write down any final things you noticed or discovered.

One past participant described her experience of choosing a spiritual teacher this way:

> I pushed back at this invitation. It is difficult for me to ask for help. I also didn't relish the idea of reading an author for it seemed an easy way for me to be cerebral and my word is *embodiment/incarnation*. After a few days I remembered bees. I remembered where my intrigue and connection with bees began or deepened. During an online retreat with Abbey of the Arts a few years ago, we were introduced to some Celtic saints. One them was Saint Gobnait for whom bees were virtually her aura for me. I enjoyed drawing her surrounded with bees. Here was ancient wisdom, here was the saint of healing (touching on embodiment and spirit) of bees; of embodied feminine mysticism. Aha, Gobnait will be my spiritual teacher in 2024. (Jane Lippert)

23

Illuminate the Word Visually

Expressive arts is a way of creating that focuses on the process over the product. It frees us to enter into the spontaneity and playfulness that creativity can offer as well as the holy surprises it sometimes brings. I like to describe my own creative practice as a journey of discovery. When I begin writing a poem, I want to follow where the poem leads rather than having it all neatly tied up before I even get started writing. The imagery, the sound of the words, the meaning will all reveal themselves as the poem unfolds.

When we work with our word through different creative media, we allow access to different ways of knowing. Visual art reveals something different from poem writing, and these are different languages from movement. We can cultivate our ability to speak in these various languages, and this will enrich our process of listening and discovery. We widen our lens and begin to see more possibilities.

Collage is a particularly accessible medium for those beginning to work with visual expression because it relies on found images rather than accessing images from within and then giving form to them.

When we work with creative expression in a prayerful context, we do so with a commitment to the process rather than the product. We are not creating for the sake of making something beautiful or perfect but to open up space on the blank page for the stirrings of our heart to have room to be made visible.

Consider this a playful time, the way you used to love drawing or creating as a child. Sometimes we can take our prayer so seriously that we forget the sacred gift of play and laughter. Play returns us to a place where we don't have to figure things out; we can simply enjoy and delight in the moment. We can follow our whimsy and pleasure.

I recommend limiting the time you take for this experience. A half hour is more than enough, and this time limit helps you to bypass your inner critic, judge, and perfectionist. If you notice those thoughts arising, meet them with compassion and bring yourself back to the inner child who delights in color and shape.

We live in a highly visual culture, bombarded at every turn by advertising—images that are designed to make us insecure or to long for whatever is being sold. When we move into working with collage as a prayer practice, we can begin to see with the eyes of the heart. We can discern which images feel life-giving and which drain us.

You can gather images from magazines, catalogs, or even old art books. Magazines like *National Geographic* work well, as the images are high-quality, less commercialized, and less sexualized, and the paper is nice quality. I find that sometimes working with just one magazine can also bring out more creativity. Instead of getting lost in an endless number of possibilities, I limit myself to one issue of something and see what it has to offer.

You will also need a circle cut out of paper or something heavier like cardboard. You can also use a cake round sold in baking supply stores or ask a local pizza restaurant if they will give you one of their unused cardboard rounds. I recommend about twelve inches in diameter. Have a glue stick and some scissors as well.

Meditation: Creating a Collage Mandala

Let this process be a prayer and a meditation. Begin with some gentle breathing and stretching to connect with your body. You might choose a piece of instrumental music to play in the background.

Then allow a few moments to center your intention. Bring your word to mind and let it guide this process. You will be making the collage intuitively, with your word as the gentlest of prompts for how to move through this creative journey. Offer up a prayer or grace you seek for this time of creation.

As you begin sorting through images, notice which ones resonate with you and which ones create a sense of dissonance. I encourage you to work with both as any image that creates a strong energetic charge, whether positive or negative, is a result of our own projection and so has some wisdom to offer us.

Allow yourself a span of time, perhaps 20–30 minutes, to let images choose you through this energetic response. Then begin placing them on the mandala in a way that feels satisfying. This is very much an intuitive process; there is no getting it "right."

When you come to the completion of your collage, allow time again to simply gaze on it before writing down your experience of the process. Have a dialogue with the images and ask what story they have to share with you. A powerful way to do this is to enter into one of the images and write the words *I am* on the page and let the image speak. Notice how it feels and experiences the world. Do this for 3–4 images and then put those images in conversation with each other. What if they were your wisdom council? How do these images reveal further dimensions of your word?

Here's what one participant, Sarah Pickering, took away from creating her mandala: "With the two words 'REST' and 'SURPRISE' in mind I headed to my pile of scraps and magazines. I loved seeing how the whole thing came together. There is nature, creating, wonder, rest, flow all involved in creating the mandala and the sun felt like the right image for the centre to hold the whole thing together."

24

Write an Acrostic Poem

You have already written a poem in the format of a pantoum, where the lines repeat in a circular way. You have been invited to lots of journaling and written reflection. Now we turn to a more condensed poetic form, the acrostic.

An acrostic poem is one in which the first letter of each line spells out a word. In the Hebrew Scriptures, the Lamentations of Jeremiah, as well as some of the proverbs and psalms, are written as acrostics of the Hebrew alphabet.

Nine of the psalms are considered acrostics, where the first letters of each line in Hebrew spell out a word that is the theme of the poem. Psalm 119 is also considered to be acrostic, but the first letter of each line moves through the Hebrew alphabet, from *aleph* to *tav*.

An acrostic can be a potent way to let your word expand and unfold into the images of the poem. The letters become signposts, directing you how to begin each line of the poem. The word itself becomes the overall theme, but you can let the lines of the poem that emerge in this process surprise you. When you feel stuck, take three slow breaths or walk away for a few minutes and look out your window. Sometimes, when I am working on a poem (or it is working on me), I take it out for a walk. New images always arise when I let my body guide the process.

Poetry also signals the mind to think in a more right-brained way. The language of poetry is not the same as the regular text. We are not trying to give instructions or directions but to let the words dance and shimmer on the page, revealing their meaning to us.

I invite you to write your own acrostic poem inspired by the word that has chosen you.

I am including a few examples here from members of our community who wrote their own poems inspired by their words. Let these serve as inspiration for your own word-inspired acrostic. Below are several examples from past participants for inspiration:

GRAVITAS

Grounded
Rooted
Alert to the present moment

Vital
In a place of peace
Thoughtful
Accompanied by the persistent presence of God
Strong
(Debbie Williams)

BREATHE

Breathe in, feel the air filling, expanding in your lungs,
Reaching down into the smallest of air sacs, deep in your being.
Exhale, let go of all that is old and past,
Ancient history consigned to a time long gone.
Train yourself to walk new paths,
Hear from Heaven itself,
Eternity begins here and now.
(Vanessa Wylie)

FLOURISH

Feel alive
Love, listen, live actively
Open myself to new experiences
Unearth hidden truths
Reconnect with forgotten dreams
Invite others in
Savor time with friends
Honor my truth
(Claire McDonald)

HUMILITY

H Heartfelt willingness to listen
U Understanding that holds and uplifts
M Mercy that bathes us all
I Insight that lands and lightens
L Love that holds and uplifts
T Tenderness that tempers each thought and action
Y Yes, Big Yes, x3, Joyfully consent each tick of the clock
(Martha Doran)

CONFIDENCE

Centered in starlight
Offering my heart openly
New insights
Found from the first
Inspiring insights
Delivered daily
Energy expanding
Never forgetting
Ceasing doubts
Everything is in me
(Martha Bartley)

Creative Practice: Write an Acrostic Poem

Write your word vertically down the page. Then allow the letters to be the prompt for the line of poetry that follows. Let the poem emerge from the process of discovery, seeing what each line wants to say as you come to it.

Writing poetry from a heart-centered place and releasing our thinking and judging minds can lead us to new places and images.

Once the poem is completed, consider posting it by your altar or somewhere you can see it on a regular basis and let it inspire you.

25

Create a Playlist of Word-Themed Songs

The great medieval abbess and visionary Hildegard of Bingen believed in the fundamental power of music to unite us with the divine. She wrote, "Therefore let everyone who understands God by faith faithfully offer Him tireless praise, and with joyful devotion sing to Him without ceasing."

Music is a sacred text through which we can encounter the holy. It is a powerful art form and has the capacity to stir the emotions and charge our memory.

Song is the primordial sound. Many traditions practice chanting and toning as ways to connect with the music that arises in the heart.

The heart chakra in Sanskrit is *anahata* and is considered to be responsible for the reception of internal music but not in the way of a normal sensory organ.

A person can listen deeply to their own inner sound through the ear of the heart, which leads to a process of spiritual awakening. The deeper one goes and experiences this primal vibration within the heart, the more one can experience it as penetrating all matter and indeed vibrating eternally throughout creation.

In yogic belief, ultimate reality emanates from the primordial first sound, the imperceptible vibration that gives rise to the universe. The entire physical world is a materialization of the different frequencies of this root vibrational energy. Human beings are also emanations of this vibration. This sound is the universal pulse of life and creation and is manifested within us as the sound of our own heart beating. For thousands of years, this primal beat has been expressed by the beat of the drum.

This image of sound energy as the fundamental creative force that is without beginning and end is similar in concept to the opening words of the Gospel according to John: “In the beginning was the Word, and the Word was with God, and the Word was God.” Similarly, in the book of Genesis, the first creation story of the Hebrew Bible, God speaks creation into being. With each act of creation, on each day of the week, is repeated the phrase “And God said,” amplifying the centrality of speech and sound to the original creation, including human beings. This calls us to remember a God whose deepest song and sound utter us into being, and we contain that sound within us. So when we enter into prayer of the heart, allowing different manifestations of this universal sound through music to be the text of our prayer, we are called into relationship with the God who sings to us and through us.

Music can be such a gift to our prayer. I imagine you have songs that lift your spirits when you hear them or songs you connect to a season of grieving or a particular memory.

The psalms are filled with descriptions of singing to God, such as "I will sing praise to your name" (9:2) and "Praise him with tambourine and dance; praise him with strings and pipe!" (150:4). All of creation is commanded to sing out: "Make a joyful noise to the Lord, all the earth. Worship the Lord with gladness; come into his presence with singing" (100:1–2). Music is a primordial sound, a powerful art form that has the capacity to stir the emotions and charge our memory.

Hildegard of Bingen composed a great deal of music to be used in praying the liturgy of the hours. We are fortunate to have many fine recordings available of her work. She believed music originated from a primordial and celestial source, and so the practice of singing was a way of joining in with this eternal choir.

Hildegard considered this form of prayer to be even more essential than the Eucharist to the formation of her community. She writes, "By this song the soul is aroused to watchfulness. . . . The song of rejoicing softens hard hearts, and draws forth tears of compunction, and invokes the Holy Spirit." Music softens our hearts so that we can make space for the Spirit to enter, and we can join with the "hidden mysteries." The music we sing is only a dim reflection of the heavenly choirs, the music from before the fall, which we could not bear in our earthly condition.

Music streaming platforms these days give us access to a lot of music, including that of Hildegard as well as Gregorian chants, if you are drawn toward explicitly sacred music. Contemporary secular music is also an appropriate and wonderful source, especially if there is a song you already love and you want to experience it in a new way. If you are like me, you already practice a form of sacred listening when you find that favorite song and play it over and over again, allowing it to shape your soul and be a channel for your emotional life. It may be a song that comes on the radio, and suddenly you find yourself emotionally connected to another time and place.

I invite you to create a playlist of songs that are connected to your word. These don't have to be songs that have your word in them but are songs that evoke the feeling quality of your word.

Creative Practice: Create a Playlist of Word-Themed Songs

To create your playlist, you might find it easiest to use an online music streaming platform. Spend some time searching for your word in song titles and seeing if any of the songs that come up feel like possible music for ongoing prayer. You can make this playlist with just three or four songs or expand it if you are finding lots of resonant music.

Then I invite you into a movement practice. Begin with a full minute of slow and deep breathing. Let your breath bring your awareness down into your body. When thoughts come up, just let them go and return to your breath. Hold your word gently in your awareness, planting a seed as you prepare to step into the dance. You don't need to think this through or figure it out; just notice what arises.

Play the songs you have chosen and let your body move in response without needing to guide the movements. Listen to how your body wants to move through space in response to your breath. Remember that this is a prayer, an act of deep listening. Pause at any time and rest in stillness again. Sit with waiting for the impulse to move and see what arises.

After the music has finished, sit for another minute in silence, connecting again to your breath. Notice your energy and any images rising up. What has been revealed about your word?

Allow another five minutes journaling in a free-writing form, just to give some space for what you are discovering.

26

Commit to a Word-Rooted Practice

Spiritual practice is a way to embody our commitments to deepening and transformation. Spirituality is not something ethereal or separate from our daily lives. Through practice, we show up and inhabit a particular way of being. Saint Benedict wrote in his Rule, "Your way of acting should be different from the world's way" (4:20). How do we show up in the world as vessels of grace and agents of divine love? The mystics tell us spiritual practice is key to our transformation.

Once a word has chosen you, consider if there is a spiritual practice that would help you to tend its unfolding in your soul for the year ahead. Keep it simple. It may be something like allowing five minutes each morning to pay attention to your breath, letting this word be a mantra or anchor for your awareness.

Commit to one regular practice that deepens your experience of this word, something that will help support you in creating space for your own continued holy birthing. Mark regular times of reflection on your calendar to look back and notice movements. The practice might be to do less of something—like watching TV or spending time on social media—and to do more of something—like spending time in silence or in nature.

If your word has still not arrived, consider if there is a spiritual practice calling to you to try. Perhaps it is one that has tugged at your heart, but you have not yet made time to deepen into it. Listen if this practice might contain the hint of a word for you for the coming year.

Meditation: Seeking Wisdom

Begin by settling into a quiet place and slowing down your breath. Bring your awareness to your heart center and rest in this inner sanctuary for a few moments in the presence of the Beloved.

Welcome in the presence of a wisdom figure; it might be Saint Benedict or another of the mystics. It might be the wisdom teacher you chose to dedicate yourself to reading during the year ahead. See who wants to arrive at the cave of your heart. Notice who appears and how they look, how you feel in their presence.

Share with them your word and any life struggles or discernment you currently have. Listen to the wisdom they offer you in response.

Then ask for their guidance for a practice you might take on for the coming months, one that would help you deepen into the insights of your word. Share with them what you long for in a practice—Do you want to feel rooted and grounded? Uplifted? Connected to nature? Spending time in silence? Being present to those beyond the veil? Deepening into Scripture? Engaging in creative expression? Movement? Speak the longings of your heart.

Listen again for their response to you. Is there a particular practice they suggest to you or other wisdom or guidance in helping you to discern?

Sit together for a while in silence. Notice if you have any other questions arising. Offer them up and again receive what is offered to you.

Before you bring this experience to completion, your wisdom teacher has a gift for you. Open your hands and receive whatever this symbol might be. Take it in, along with what its meaning for you might be. Bring your body into a shape or gesture that embodies this symbol and breathe into it, letting it inhabit you.

Offer a bow of gratitude and know you can return here at any time. Slowly bring your awareness back to the room you are in and allow some time for journaling any new insights or discoveries. Make a commitment to your spiritual practice.

Past participants gathered these insights from the meditation:

> Some aspects of ourselves are covered over by our verbal self we draw in the right brain, wordlessly, and drawings, therefore, show us how we see things and feel about them. Some of the verbal processes have distorted my thinking regarding the "not good enough" theme. Learning to draw and paint never ends.
>
> I would like to set myself to practice drawing/painting a little each day, so I may not lose my taste for it.
>
> No matter how little it is, it is well worthwhile, and it does me a world of good. (Sandra Johnston)

> As I thought about a daily word-rooted practice, *breath* came first to mind. Currently, I am an exerciser; seldom do I miss a day of running, biking, or some other form of vigorous physical activity. Connecting to my breath is something for me to practice more, as it will help me to "take a deep breath" when accepting may be a struggle. A daily deliberate practice of meditation, quiet yoga, or reading a poem from my spiritual teacher (Mary Oliver) to balance every physical workout is a word-rooted practice that feels right for me and will support letting go of anger, hurt, or judgment and showing up with joy and gratitude. (Paulette Thabault)

27

Write a Seven-Word Prayer

We are nearing the end of this journey together. It has been a pilgrimage of sorts, in daily life. I sometimes describe pilgrimage as a journey that courts holy disruption. When we are tourists, we arrive to a place seeking prepackaged experiences that run on time and don't make us uncomfortable.

When we are pilgrims, we open our hearts to those moments of holy disruption as the places where we might be expanded past the confines of how we live our lives.

For several years before the pandemic, my husband, John, and I led pilgrimage experiences in Ireland, Germany, and Austria. We sometimes invited people to write a seven-word prayer as we began. This was a practice of reflecting on their heart's desire for this journey. People often come on pilgrimage when they are at a threshold in their lives and are seeking discernment.

Perhaps you are at your own life threshold. Certainly, the start of a new year brings its own sense of fresh energy and new possibilities. Even the ending of this formal journey through the reflections here is a transition time. The season ahead is a new kind of pilgrimage through daily life.

You have already been invited to create a breath prayer to weave into your days to come. This prayer is one you could write on the cover of your journal or put on your screensaver on your phone or computer. You could write this on an index card and tape it to your mirror. There are many ways this could accompany you through the ordinary moments of your life.

Sometimes when I feel a bit unmoored, a simple line of prayer can act as an anchor, returning me to center. I love putting it in a couple of places so that I will come across it regularly. It helps me remember my commitment and practice.

If you wanted to carry a prayer with you for this year that helped remind you to deepen into this word, what might it be? Seven is a sacred number and helps you get to the essence of things.

If your prayer really wants to be six or eight or even ten words long, trust that. There is no way to get this wrong. This is an act of discernment, listening for the essential words that help you express the prayer at the heart of the word you have received. Everything we have been doing here is a prayer to connect to our own deepest selves and to the divine, however we understand that loving presence in our lives.

Meditation: Write a Seven-Word Prayer

As a way of naming the grace you seek for this time, I invite you to open yourself to receive a seven-word prayer to carry with you. Notice what the prayer of your heart is for this time and which words or images seem to draw you forward. Seven is a sacred number in religious traditions and also requires that you return to the essence of what you long for—no extraneous words necessary. Let this evolve over several days, sitting with whether the words that have emerged feel right for you.

Write your word for the year on the page and then write other words around it, like a mind map. Let free associations arise. Then slowly craft your prayer from these fragments.

Once it has landed—offered a sense of rightness in your being—let this be your mantra for the time ahead. Much like praying with prayer beads or a holy word in centering prayer, the mantra can be a focus and its repetition a source of comfort. Repeat it gently to yourself several times during the day. Consider writing it in your journal and maybe on a sticky note by your computer or up on your mirror so it greets you each day. Say it in moments of transition from one activity to another, for these are threshold spaces, times that are especially ripe for leaning into sacred awareness.

Be inspired by these seven-word (or five-word or eight-word) prayers from past participants:

> Establish us deep in Love. (Sally Nettles)
>
> Open to the wisdom of resistance. (Lois Perron)
>
> Lord, help me dance into DELIGHT today. (Lynne Jensen)
>
> Accept, have joy and gratitude, I pray. (Paulette Thabault)
>
> Let me sing to you on HOLY ground. (Nancy Husk)
>
> God I ask you to fill me. (Kimberly Cortner)
>
> My prayer as haiku (word: Awakening)
>
> Grateful for the growth that is
>
> Slowly simmering
>
> Prayer for guidance and more
>
> (Carrie Jalonen)
>
> My life is fire. Be the wind. (Kimber Court Del Valle)
>
> My word is *expand*. Source of All, help me expand my life. (Kerry Howarth)

28

Create a Simple Word-Centered Rule of Life

Many monastic and other religious communities have a "rule of life" as part of the foundation of their community life. The Rule of Benedict is probably one of the best-known rules; it was written in the sixth century and continues to guide Benedictines around the world 1,500 years later. It is especially valued for its wisdom and sense of balance. Some religious rules can be harsh and strict, but Benedict always strived for balance.

These rules can be wisdom guides for healthy and balanced living that also fosters creativity. The creative life requires this gentle tension between freedom and structure or spontaneity and limitations. This is where a rule of life can be helpful, providing a gentle trellis of structure for our lives. When approached with freedom and playfulness, boundaries can help spark our creativity.

As human beings seeking to live meaningful lives, we hunger for some kind of structure, a set of practices that challenge us and help us grow. Yet, if our rule is too rigorous, we can become suffocated by legalism. The paradox of the spiritual life is that it needs a healthy balance of structure and freedom to thrive. This is the paradox of the creative process as well.

Beyond the creative act itself, I find there are certain rhythms to my life that are essential for my creative energy. These include writing each morning, walking to care for my body, letting my energy shift out of my head for a while, knowing when to let go and let something incubate, and getting adequate rest and play. The balance of the Benedictine life is most conducive to my creative life. Of course, there are many other systems and traditions one could follow, and the purpose of the rule is to grow in our awareness of the holy presence. If creativity is one of the ways in which we reflect the Creator, then a rule of life that nurtures our creativity is one that can also help us to grow spiritually.

A rule of life is essentially a reflective commitment on specific practices you want to incorporate into your regular routine. A rule is meant to be balanced and not out of reach. It should not make you feel guilty for not living up to it, so aim for a rule of moderation. If you find the word *rule* difficult, you might imagine it as a trellis—a balance of structure and open space through which you can grow, offering boundaries while remaining open-ended and flexible. You do not have to write your "once-and-for-all-forever-rule-of-life." In fact, I encourage you to reflect regularly, perhaps at each transition to a new season, and notice whether your rule is providing too little or too much structure for you.

Meditation: Writing Your Word-Inspired Rule

A rule of life is essentially a document that is broken down into several wide categories that encourage balance. Let your word for the year be your foundation and guide for creating this trellis.

Consider some of the following questions when writing your rule:

Which prayer practices nourish you? What would be a sustainable commitment to prayer for you daily, weekly, monthly, seasonally, annually?

What commitments to yourself do you want to make? Where are your areas of further growth? Where would you like to deepen your practice? What are your growing edges right now?

What relationships in your life do you want to cultivate—relationships with self, family, friends, community, nature, global concerns, God? What commitments might you make to contribute to their flourishing?

Perhaps keep your rule limited to three principles or guidelines. These can be very specific, such as pray with Scripture daily or go for a contemplative walk each day, carrying your word with you. Or they can be more general, such as find moments to bring compassion to yourself and others or create time and space for creative pursuits. Let your word guide you in each of these principles. How does your word offer you insight about the commitments you want to make?

Past participants produced these rules:

My rule is called "Launch into the Deep" . . . a commitment to daily and seasonal practices . . . one practice is to be mindful and open to moments of wonder. (Anne)

Weekly walks in the woods, full moon creativity nights, checking in quarterly. (Melissa PN)

Be open to the glimmers of Daily Delights and bursts of light that bring light and joy in the world. Prayer, dance, journal and share my God Delights with others. My delight yesterday was my granddaughter chasing the rainbows from the light coming through the windows. (Lynne Jensen)

My word is "unleash" (and "release" as the counterbalance), each month I hope to listen to what element of myself yearns to be unleashed—then each day will surge in my body for three minutes (sprint, bike, row, stretch) and create around what I am unleashing (a song, poem, strum, drum, etc.) however I am led. (Angela Wolle)

29

Practice *Lectio Divina* with Revelation 2:17

Let anyone who has an ear listen to what the Spirit is saying to the churches. To everyone who conquers I will give some of the hidden manna, and I will give a white stone, and on the white stone is written a new name that no one knows except the one who receives it. (REVELATION 2:17)

You are invited into the practice of *lectio divina*, or sacred reading, with the text from Revelation above. Even if you have read a Scripture text dozens of times before, with this practice, you meet it as if it were new, as if it were being spoken into your life at this very moment in new ways. Which indeed it is.

This story has a powerful image of the gift of a white stone with a new name written on it. What if this new name were your word?

Preparation

A helpful place to begin is with your breath, slowing and deepening it and allowing it to bring you as fully present to this moment as possible.

As you settle into the rhythm of the breath, see if you can draw your awareness from your head down to your heart center. You might even place your hand on your heart to create a physical connection. Spend a few moments to simply rest here, feeling whatever the truth of your experience is in this moment, allowing it to have space. Then bring to your awareness what the mystics tell us—that the infinite compassion of God dwells within our hearts. Breathe in this infinite Source of Compassion and allow it to fill you in this moment.

First Movement—Lectio: *Settling and Shimmering*

Begin by finding a comfortable position where you can remain alert and yet also relax your body. Bring your attention to your breath and allow a few moments to become centered. If you find yourself distracted at any time, gently return to the rhythm of your breath as an anchor for your awareness. Allow yourself to settle into this moment and become fully present.

Read the passage above from Revelation once or twice through, slowly, and listen for a word or phrase that feels significant right now, that is capturing your attention even if you don't know why. Gently repeat this word to yourself in the silence.

Second Movement—Meditatio: *Savoring and Stirring*

Read the text again and then allow the word or phrase that caught your attention in the first movement to spark your imagination. Savor the word or phrase with all of your senses; notice which smells, sounds, tastes, sights, and feelings are evoked. Then listen for which images, feelings, and memories are stirring, welcoming them in, and then savor and rest into this experience.

Third Movement—Oratio: *Summoning and Serving*

Read the text a third time and then listen for an invitation rising up from your experience of prayer so far. Considering the word or phrase and what it has evoked for you in memory, image, or feeling, what is the invitation? This invitation may be a summons toward a new awareness or action.

Fourth Movement—Contemplatio: *Slowing and Stilling*

Move into a time for simply resting in God and allowing your heart to fill with gratitude for God's presence in this time of prayer. Slow your thoughts and reflections even further and sink into the experience of stillness. Rest in the presence of God and allow yourself to simply be. Rest here for several minutes. Return to your breath if you find yourself distracted.

Closing

Gently connect with your breath again and slowly bring your awareness back to the room, moving from inner experience to outer experience. Give yourself some time of transition between these moments of contemplative depth and your everyday life. Consider taking a few minutes to journal about what you experienced in your prayer.

For example, if I were to pray with this passage from Revelation, I would read it through twice to begin, listening for the word or phrase that shimmers. In this reading now, *on the white stone is written a new name* is calling to me. I might speak the words aloud to hear them. I let them echo for a moment in my heart.

I read the text again and now let that phrase unfold within me. I welcome in feelings of awe and reverence, memories of moments when the holy erupted in unexpected ways into my life, and an image of a smooth stone waiting to be etched with new possibility.

I read the text one more time and listen now for the invitation. Today, it is to carry this word with me into the year ahead as a sacred treasure that holds secrets I have yet to discover. I close with some time in silence and then journal any insights that emerged.

30

Go Forward into a New Season

Give me a small line of verse from time to time, oh God, and if I cannot write it down for lack of paper or light, then let me address it softly in the evening to your Great Heaven.

But please give me a small line of verse now and then.

—Etty Hillesum, *An Interrupted Life*

I open this final day of practice with a quote from Etty Hillesum, a twentieth-century Dutch Jewish mystic. This longing and deep desire for a word to illuminate us go back centuries, even as far back as the desert elders I wrote about in the first few days of our practice together.

This sense of intimacy with words was cultivated early on in relationship to sacred texts of Scripture but also referred to all the ways the divine offers us a word to help guide us into the next season of life.

With the practice of sacred reading, or *lectio divina*, the ancient desert fathers and mothers believed that the Hebrew and Christian Scriptures were like a love letter written to us by God. They are living and animated in an ongoing way by the Spirit. The texts speak to us in this unique moment of our lives, wherever we find ourselves. Each time we come to the text, we are in a new place, and the text responds directly to what is happening in this moment. *Lectio* assumes that God speaks to us intimately in the unique circumstances of our lives, responding in new ways to each moment.

We can say the same of the words that arrive into our lives, whether through the gift of a revered elder, a dream, an intuition, or synchronicity—these holy words offer an unending mystery, meaning we can never exhaust the depth of their meaning. We can pray with this word throughout the year ahead because it continues to offer us its gifts and graces again and again.

The Holy One is already praying in us. Through this practice of receiving a word, we make ourselves available to join this unceasing prayer already happening in our hearts. God is the one who initiates the dialogue. Our practice is to make space to hear this prayer already at work within us. This is not intellectual knowledge but heart wisdom.

What is necessary for this prayer is a willingness to surrender yourself to the process. The thinking mind will try to control what unfolds or analyze and judge what is happening. The heart is the place of receptivity, integration, and meaning-making. It is where thinking, feeling, intuition, and wisdom come together. In this process, we are called to nothing short of transformation.

Another thing I deeply value about this practice is how two or more people might receive the same word for the year, and yet each person will have a unique experience that rises up out of their own life context in that moment.

When I encounter and receive the word, I bring all of my memories and relationships, my feelings and dreams to the word or phrase that has arrived.

To close out this set of practices, I invite you into a simple ritual. First, you will need a stone of some kind. If you have a white one, that will evoke the reading from Revelation we prayed with on day 29, but any color will be fine. Perhaps look for one from your local geology. A smooth stone will make for easier writing. You will also need a permanent marking pen in a color of your choosing.

Creative Practice: Write Your Word on a Stone

I invite you to commit a half hour or more to a closing ritual for this journey. Gather your stone and pen and set up an altar space with a candle and cloth. You may already have an altar, or you might like to create one just for this experience. Bring your collage, your pantoum, your acrostic poem, your seven-word prayer, and your rule of life as well. Perhaps there are some other symbols you might like to add that feel important, whether an icon, an element of nature, or some other items that help evoke the spirit of your word for you.

Begin by lighting a candle and sitting in silence for a few minutes, praying the breath prayer you created the other day. Hold an intention of listening to the Spirit. Then behold what you have created in this time and bring a sense of loving reverence. Read through the poems and rule and notice what is stirred. Gaze on your collage and see if any new insights emerge.

Hold a sense of gratitude for this journey and for all that is still to come as your word continues to reveal its gifts over time. You might want to journal for a while to reflect on any new insights that have been arriving.

Hold the stone in your hands; feel its weight and density. Connect to its presence, letting it be an anchor for you to this moment. Bless the stone. Read the Scripture passage from Revelation again: "Let anyone who has an ear listen to what the Spirit is saying to the churches. To everyone who conquers I will give some of the hidden manna, and I will give a white stone, and on the white stone is written a new name that no one knows except the one who receives it" (Revelation 2:17).

With your marking pen, write your word on the stone in a prayerful way. Receive this word as a new name for this season of life. Listen for the blessing being offered to you.

Place this stone somewhere you will see it regularly—perhaps on your altar, on your desk, or another place—as a reminder to return to your word throughout the year.

Postlude

Distillation

Some years, my word comes quickly, and some years, it demands a lot more listening and waiting until I receive it. Sometimes I feel certain the word is shimmering, and other times I am uncertain and so hold whatever seems to come lightly and with openness.

The first half of 2022 was a challenge for my health. I started with COVID-19 in January; then my very dear aunt died suddenly, and I was unable to be with her at her passing; and in March 2022, I traveled to Vienna, Austria, to have major surgery.

I had a quiet summer, resting and recovering slowly. I traveled in September to Slovenia, a trip that was originally postponed due to the pandemic and a place where one of my ancestral lines came from. When I returned from that trip, however, I got quite sick with a bronchial virus for two weeks. Following that, some other medical issues emerged and flared.

Nothing life-threatening, thankfully, but things were challenging.

I was working with my doctor to explore various options. I also cleared a lot of space for myself. I rested a great deal and was allowing myself to be with all that my body was saying to me. It was sweet as well to open even more to the grief over losing my aunt and feeling her and my mother keenly present with me in this challenging season.

I share this whole litany of ailments not for sympathy; we all have our vulnerable seasons, and our contemplative practice is not a shield against struggle. It can certainly help in coping and enduring and discovering the grace at the heart of it all, but it will never exempt us from our humanity.

That whole year, I had been meditating a lot with the Black Madonna in the form of Our Lady of the Underworld and with Sister Death (named so affectionately by Saint Francis)—both for my aunt who crossed that threshold and for myself as I certainly have a lot of living I still want to do, but I feel drawn like those ancient monks to remember my fragility and to let that bring a luminosity to my days. Benedict instructs us to "keep death daily before your eyes" (RB 4:47).

The underworld journey—sometimes called *the dark night of the soul*—comes for each of us and is ultimately in service of stripping away our old attachments and coming to greater clarity about what is ours to do in this world and how we are to be.

Each morning, I wake so grateful for the gift of another day of loving, of watching the light change through the hours, of pondering the big questions of life. Even those days when I have to spend much of it horizontal, I open my heart to dream time and trust that, in this fallowness, a newness will eventually emerge.

I think part of this is certainly being in that menopausal season and passing fifty a few years ago. Both my parents died in their early sixties, so there is an intensifying desire in me to live fully even when that sometimes means just taking one breath at a time.

One of the greatest gifts of this season is this sense of harvesting and distilling the abundance of my life—my years of study and practice, the struggles and times of wrestling. As we get older, if we are paying attention, that which we no longer need is stripped away. Sometimes this happens in a slow, willing release on our part, and sometimes there is a sudden stripping. This is part of death and the underworld's gift to us, plunging into the essence of what feels most vital in our lives. When we come to realize how time is fleeting, we can let go of that which no longer brings us alive. Time is also slow and spacious, and we can nurture that expansiveness by slowing down and bringing full attention to it all.

I was listening to a talk online, and one of the women speaking used the word *distillation*. When I heard it, it shimmered for me. It made something flutter inside me, a certain sense of rightness, a yes to this holy direction. That is sometimes how the word arrives. You pray, and you open, and you discern, and then suddenly you hear someone say something that may have nothing to do with your prayers, but a single word shines in the midst of it all.

Distillation for me means continuing to lavish my body with care, nourishing my friendships and support system with time and care, and also tending to my beautiful community, the work of my heart.

Death and life are intimately intertwined—the old and the new braided together. We live in what feels like end times, but emerging all around us is a new vision as well.

Blessing for New Beginnings

We call on the Holy One of newness
who reveals all that is fresh and alive and wondrous,
bless us as we cross this threshold
into a new beginning.
May the word that has arrived to our inner shores
glimmer and guide the way into the season ahead.
In moments of uncertainty, let the word be an anchor,
in times of grief, let the word carve out space in us
to lament and weep,
in times of celebration, let the word confirm
all that is good and beautiful in our lives.
Let this word call us back always to Love,
echoing our heart's deepest desires.
Let it weave its way through
all the holy ordinary moments
so that we might remember our wholeness
and respond with generosity to a world in need.
May you be blessed and a blessing to others.

Acknowledgments

Every book is a collaborative effort. From the seeds of this work, inspired by the wisdom of those fierce and wise desert mothers and fathers. To the creative Spirit at work every time I sit down to put words on a page. To the endless gifts of cups of tea and loving support while writing from my husband, John, and the steady presence my dog, Sourney, provides. To the enthusiastic engagement with the developing materials over the years by our wondrous dancing monks community. To the encouragement for this work by the Broadleaf team and the keen editing of Lisa Kloskin. And now in your hands, dearest reader, the one I have been writing for all along. May it open some new doorway inside you.

For all of this, my heart overflows with gratitude.

Notes

Introduction

xii *"he or she is not asking for either a command or a solution"*: Rowan Williams, *Silence and Honey Cakes* (Lion Books, 2004), 50.

xii *"'Sit in your cell,'"*: Benedicta Ward, SLG, trans., *The Sayings of the Desert Fathers* (Cistercian Publications, 1975), 104.

xii *"A monk once came to Basil of Caesarea"*: Benedicta Ward, trans., introduction to *Sayings of the Desert Fathers* (Cistercian Publications, 1975), xxii.

2 *"This familiar life and body"*: Stephanie Dowrick, *In the Company of Rilke: Why a 20th-Century Visionary Poet Speaks So Eloquently to 21st-Century Readers* (Penguin Publishing Group, 2009), Kindle.

3 *"to give oneself over to the enjoyment"*: WordReference.com, last accessed November 1, 2024, Online Language Dictionaries, English Dictionary.

Chapter 2: Listen with the Heart

13 *"In the innermost depths of my heart"*: Kallistos Ware, *Paths to the Heart: Sufism and the Christian East* (World Wisdom Books, 2003), 9.

14 ***Saint Benedict begins his rule***: Timothy Fry, OSB, ed., *RB 1980: The Rule of St. Benedict* in English (Liturgical Press, 1981), 15.

Chapter 6: Give Me One Wild Word

35 ***"Give me one wild word"***: Terry Tempest Williams, *Finding Beauty in a Broken World* (Vintage Books, 2009), 2.

Chapter 7: Tend the Night Wisdom of Dreams

39 ***From Joseph of the Old Testament***: Genesis 37:1–44.

39 ***Jacob's dream of a staircase from earth to heaven***: Genesis 28:10–17.

39 ***Daniel's dream of the four beasts***: Daniel 7:1–14.

40 ***being told not to be afraid to take pregnant Mary***: Matthew 1:20–21.

40 ***Joseph is then warned in a dream to leave Bethlehem***: Matthew 2:13.

40 ***Joseph is told that it is safe to go back to Israel***: Matthew 2:19–20.

40 ***he departed for the region of Galilee instead***: Matthew 2:22.

45 ***"Go forth and eat nothing until you get"***: Edward Sellner, *Stories of the Celtic Soul Friends: Their Meaning for Today* (Paulist Press, 2004), 7.

Chapter 8: Consult a Soul Friend

46 ***"The relationship of soul-friendship existed between men and women"***: Esther De Waal, *The Celtic Way of Prayer* (The Crown Publishing Group, 1999), Kindle.

47 ***There are many ways to find a spiritual direction*:** Consider checking with your church or the website of Spiritual Directors International (https://www.sdicompanions.org/). Look for the *find* button on their menu bar.

57 ***"Keep death daily before one's eyes"*:** Leonard J. Doyle, trans., *Saint Benedict's Rule for Monasteries* (Order of Saint Benedict, 1948, 2001), 47.

Chapter 10: Imagine Your Deathbed

58 ***"Facing death gives our loving force, clarity, and focus"*:** Alan Jones, *Soul Making: The Desert Way of Spirituality* (HarperCollins, 1985), 60.

Interlude: Surplus

64 ***"Nothing happens, which is enough to frighten any modern person"*:** Robert Johnson, *The Fisher King and the Handless Maiden* (HarperCollins, 1995), 93.

Chapter 11: Allow the Word to Ripen

71 ***"In my ripening / ripens / what you are"*:** Rainer Maria Rilke, *Book of Hours: Love Poems to God*, trans. Anita Barrows and Joanna Macy (Riverhead Books, 1996), ii, 15, 115.

Chapter 12: Trust What You Love

77 ***"It is said that all you are seeking is also seeking you"*:** Clarissa Pinkola Estes, *Women Who Run with the Wolves* (Ballantine Books, 1995), 149.

77 ***"Don't ask yourself what the world needs"*:** Lerita Coleman Brown, *What Makes You Come Alive* (Broadleaf Books, 2023), 7.

78 ***"This most of all: ask yourself in the most silent hour"*:** Rainer Maria Rilke, *Letters to a Young Poet*, trans. M. D. Herter Norton (Norton, 2004), 16.

79 ***"Do not give your heart to that which does not satisfy"*:** Sr. Benedicta Ward, trans., *The Sayings of the Desert Fathers* (Cistercian Publications, 1975), 178.

Chapter 16: Attune to Your Body's Wisdom

98 ***the body is the last unexplored wilderness*:** Reginald Ray, *Touching Enlightenment* (Sounds True, 2014), 12.

Chapter 19: Call on the Angels, Saints, and Ancestors

114 ***"They mark the path with their wisdom"*:** Joyce Rupp, *Fragments of Your Ancient Name: 365 Glimpses of the Divine for Daily Meditation* (Sorin Books, 2011), entry for November 1.

Interlude: Hermit

127 ***"I need to be silent for a while"*:** Daniel Ladinsky, *Love Poems to God: Twelve Sacred Voices from the East and West* (Penguin Books, 2002), 112.

Chapter 21: Create a Breath Prayer

131 ***"pray without ceasing"*:** 1 Thessalonians 5:16.

132 ***"Let the name of Jesus adhere to your breath"*:** Philokalia: The Eastern Christian Spiritual Texts, annotated by Allyne Smith (SkyLight Paths Publishing, 2006), 167.

Chapter 25: Create a Playlist of Word-Themed Songs

153 ***"Therefore let everyone who understands God"*:** Hildegard of Bingen, *Scivias*, trans. Mother Columba Hart and Jane Bishop (Paulist Press, 1990), 534.

156 ***"By this song the soul"*:** Hildegard of Bingen: Scivias, trans., Mother Columba Hart and Jane Bishop (Classics of Western Spirituality) (Paulist Press, 1990) (Book Three, Vision Thirteen, 13–14), 534.

Postlude: Distillation

186 ***"keep death daily before your eyes"*:** Judith Sutera, OSB, *St. Benedict's Rule: An Inclusive Translation and Daily Commentary* (Liturgical Press, 2021), 51.